Since gaining his taste for travel in Europe and Australia as a young man, Steve Willis has travelled the world extensively – for pleasure with his family, and during his career as a businessman and management consultant … though never again in a tent!

Steve is a Londoner by birth who has lived in Australia almost continuously for the last 35 years, apart from a two-and-a-half year stint in Hong Kong, to keep things interesting. He is married to Jenny and has two grown up children, Nick and Katy, all of whom remind him how little he actually knows, on a regular basis.

He is fortunate to call the beautiful harbour city of Sydney home.

Europe over the Handlebars

One Brit, one Aussie,
four wheels and five countries

STEVE WILLIS

BROADCAST

First published in Australia in 2021 by Steve Willis
comms4handlebars@gmail.com

A catalogue record for this work is available from the National Library of Australia

ISBN: 978-0-6452373-4-4 (Paperback)

Produced by Broadcast Books, www.broadcastbooks.com.au
Edited by Paul Anderson and Bernadette Foley
Proofread by Puddingburn Publishing
Cover and text design by Christabella Designs
Typeset in Garamond 11.5/16pt by Christabella Designs
Cover photographs by Steve and Jenny Willis
Printed by The SOS Print + Media Group (Aust) Pty Ltd

To my European cycling and life partner, Jenny,
for inspiring me to finally write this story.

And to our grown-up children, Nick and Katy,
who inspire me every day,
with their passion to make things better.

Contents

FIRENZE
Firenze

FIRENZE
Firenze

Prologue

As we rounded the fortieth corner, toiling up a mountain that we thought would never end, and dodged the speeding Fiats, driven by madly waving Italians coming towards us, Passo del Bracco seemed a long way from the Italian Riviera we had left earlier that morning – and even further from our homes in London and Sydney.

'I'm enjoying the experience of climbing this mountain with no first or second gear,' I called out to Jenny, between gasps for breath. It was my own fault, as I'd made a complete pig's ear of adjusting the derailleur on my bike earlier that day.

This wasn't quite what I had expected to be doing in June of 1984, but then I was learning to appreciate the unexpected. Only the previous year, I was minding my own business, enjoying a quiet pint at our favourite watering hole in Pinner, after an early season rugby session, when Jenny, my Aussie girlfriend, decided to shatter the calm.

'So, let's cycle around Europe then,' she said.

Six words that took some time to digest for someone who, up to that point, had viewed bikes as a useful but last-ditch form of transport – for the paper round as a boy; getting to work as a young man; and more recently, getting to and from the pub when there was no car to borrow. After all, this was London in the early 1980s, and if you were over eighteen and riding a bike on the road, in the suburbs where I grew up, it was generally assumed that you were doing so because you couldn't afford a car. Bikes hadn't yet achieved the socially acceptable status created by 'middle-aged men in lycra' (mamils) and other round wheel fitness disciples of the twenty-first century.

So I was naturally asking myself, How did we get here? To find the answer, I merely needed to cast my mind back to 1981 and a sawdust-strewn pub in London Wall, where the seeds for this European adventure were unwittingly being sown by a Scotsman. It may seem a cliché for an Englishman to point the finger of blame at a Scotsman, but in this instance, I think you'll find the target is justified.

I had hatched a plan with this fellow escapee from merchant banking boredom – to head for America, meander south to catch a boat to the West Indies and, when our funds ran dry, fly to Australia where we could use our recently acquired working visas to replenish our coffers. As with many of the best plans, the devil is in the detail, which became apparent when my fellow traveller came to work one day with some unexpected news.

'I've been selected to represent Scotland in the Commonwealth Games next year in Brisbane.'

'Congratulations and good for you!' I replied.

Then realisation slowly dawned – he'd be going Down Under without passing through America or the West Indies and, inconveniently for my trip, he was the one with contacts in both locations.

Having told most of the people I knew that I was heading off on this adventure, including my employer, who showed more keenness for the idea than I would have liked, I wasn't about to bail out at that point. So, it was Australia for me. Rugby friends and immediate family were surprised, to say the least, at this new-found passion for the sunburnt country when I announced, rather grandly, that I was now intending to work and live in Australia for twelve months. They wanted to know what possessed me to plan this trip. When, well before the internet or any other instant feedback loop, the average English person's impression of Australia was of a distant continent – full of abrasive cricketers, a kangaroo called Skippy capable of solving complex crimes, and lots of critters bent on killing you. In fact, it seemed to us that almost anything there that crawled, slithered or swam wanted to end your life.

There were indeed many harmful creatures in Oz when I arrived in 1982, even in suburban Sydney. But what I also found was a country that was environmentally unique, rapidly shedding its cultural cringe, and with a real can-do attitude. Especially when compared to the more divided and socially troubled societies in the UK and much of Europe in the early 1980s. It was energising. Also – and starting to get to the point for this diversion in time – for a red-blooded twenty-two year-old from Harrow, it had one other notable characteristic that meant it was a match made in heaven: there appeared to be tanned and attractive young women everywhere I went. Especially in Manly, where I was living in an apartment on the beachfront. And it was there, at a time when I was supposed to be tooling around America or the Caribbean, that I met one of those athletic Aussie goddesses and my European cycling companion-to-be. So, as I said, I mostly blame the Scotsman.

I did, however, graciously accept some blame myself, for the afore-mentioned cycling trip. I was supposed to be on a carefree trip around the world in 1982. But I became emotionally involved with this fit and very active twenty-two year-old Australian who, having come to the UK after we met in Sydney, was determined to see and do as much as possible in her two years in Blighty. And Jenny's family did have the adventurer's gene. Her grandfather had flown Sopwith Camels as a squadron leader over the trenches of France during the latter stages of the First World War and had been an aviation pioneer. Now, while it's true that Italian drivers especially can be dangerous to share roads with on a pushbike – and we were going to be heavily laden and on the *wrong* side of the road – compared to the prospect of being shot down with no parachute over enemy territory, we weren't exactly risking our lives. Maybe just the odd limb.

Meanwhile, back in 1983 in that Pinner pub, I found myself contemplating a pedal-powered trip around Europe the following year. It wasn't that I was reluctant to go, or that I was concerned about fitness – I played rugby, ran most days and was still in good physical shape after twelve months in Oz and six months travelling home under my own steam. And, at six foot three inches and fourteen and a half stones, I was more than capable of generating sufficient pedal power for the trip. However, my view of cycling was that there were better ways to get fit. And now that I could drive and was grown up, I wasn't sure that I wanted to reacquaint myself intimately with that form of transport over an extended period. So, I was still struggling to get my head around how we had moved, in the space of one conversation, from my initial suggestion to Jenny: 'Let's buy a second-hand Kombi van and drive around Europe.'

Of course, with the benefit of hindsight, once we started planning a European trip and doing the research, we were always heading that way, with our, shall we say, constrained financial status. It was true that plenty of antipodeans still thought the iconic Kombi was a key part of their rite of passage around Europe – a short stroll from the Caledonian Road tube station in Islington, to an unofficial second-hand Kombi market, would confirm that. However, it also quickly became obvious, as we looked at the prices, that by the time we had bought it, kitted it out and paid for petrol on the way round the continent, we could only afford a month and we'd be eating like wartime refugees on food rations along the way. Efficient but the opposite of the experience we were chasing. Rail travel was also not going to cut it if we wanted to experience out-of-the-way places and be able to move around wherever and whenever the mood took us.

But, by bike, I was reliably informed by my future cycling companion, we would have the flexibility to go where we wanted and could be away on that magical continent for up to five months. Of course, the logic of extending the time there, while being propelled by nothing but our own lungs and legs, hadn't really entered that discussion – after all, we were planning to head mainly down river valleys and along the coast and it all looked pretty flat on our *Collins Road Atlas of Europe*. We probably should have bought the Michelin maps with helpful contours before we went to France, rather than rely on a very large map book designed for cars. But hey, we were young, fit and indestructible. What could possibly go wrong?

So, it was settled. It seemed we would climb onto our yet-to-be-purchased bikes and pedal around Europe – carrying the tent, panniers, camping gear, maps, clothes and … a very red pair of high-heeled shoes, which mysteriously made it into the bottom of *my* panniers, but we'll get to that later.

But, before we could get to Europe, we had to move from idea to action. It was September 1983 and the year in Britain had been politically turbulent, to say the least; and Europe had not fared much better. However, despite predictions to the contrary, it seemed that at least we wouldn't be tracked everywhere by the totalitarian Eurasian state of Orwell's imagination, when we planned to tour there in 1984. In fact, the countries we wanted to visit on our loop through Europe – France, Italy, Switzerland, Germany, and the Netherlands – didn't appear much closer to complete unity, as far as we could tell from our vantage point in Britain.

So, we had to plan to travel through five quite different and independent countries ... very slowly. Time to draw on some of those adventurer genes from Jenny's family, it seemed.

CHAPTER 1
Planning and getting organised

As relative European novices, we figured we should do a bit of research rather than just turn up and wing it – which was the unhelpful advice of many of my rugby mates. So, before we invested in our new transport and portable home, and after buying the obligatory pocket phrasebook, we decided to make three other important purchases to help us in our planning and to take on our trip.

The first of these was the *AA Book of Camping and Caravanning*, written by that very fine institution, with a long tradition of providing invaluable travel and roadside services to its members. The AA assured us they had inspected four thousand sites to create this book. They also threw in their views on 'the best of Europe's beaches', advice for camping equipment, tent preparation, and many other nuggets of wisdom as part of the deal. We decided that we didn't need their thoughts on how to properly tow a boat, caravan or trailer. But the checklist for camping equipment, making phone calls from Europe to the UK, and exchanging money did prove to be very useful for these two novices. They also suggested that: 'Apart from observing local regulations, you are strongly advised not to camp by the roadside and in isolated areas.' Thanks for the warning. We agreed and had no such plans, but this handy tome did save us several times from exactly that fate.

Looking back now, from a time of online information overload, we were fortunate in 1983, as we were planning our trip, that the quality of the reviews and information was professionally prepared, understandable and overwhelmingly reliable. Especially when compared to the grammatically suspect and often unreliable entries contributed by some of the intellectual giants of today to online travel sites. Where comments on Italy include such helpful gems as: 'Apparently Rome has not yet discovered building maintenance. The *coloseam* [sic] was very rundown and did not have any refreshment stands or cleaning crew of *any kind*.'

No shit, Sherlock – that's probably because it's two thousand years old and, that's sort of the point. What I want to know is, why are these people even allowed out in public, let alone to comment on a site that gives advice to others. Also, where's Russell Crowe when you need him?

Current online travel services do seem easier and more accessible, but sorting through the dross to get to the genuine reviews can be exhausting.

Our second important purchase was the *Collins Road Atlas of Europe*. Given we were spending our time on bikes and carrying everything with us, we possibly should have thought this through a little longer. The map book was 15 by 12 inches, when fully closed, which wasn't going to be ideal for the handlebars of a bike or storing in our panniers. It was also going to be our main source of information until we found Michelin guides in Europe. It was, however, very useful to work through our initial options and it did helpfully include an 'Index to 39,000 place names, city plans and through routes'. Although, the latter were mostly autobahns and motorways, which we definitely weren't going to be using. But in 1983, the choice of European maps, though abundant for motorists, was a little more underwhelming for hardy cyclists who planned to travel using smaller back roads.

In reality, our route plan was quite high level. It might even have been described as a triumph of optimism over practicality, but at least we had a plan. We were going to ferry to France, catch the train to Paris to see some friends and then on to Lyon, where we would start cycling at the top of the classic Rhône Valley – *Route de vin.* We would then make our way down to Marseille; through the French and Italian Rivieras; a quick detour through Florence, down to Rome and up to Venice; pop over the Alps through Switzerland; zigzag up the Rhine Valley to the Netherlands and finish in Amsterdam. All before returning to the welcoming arms of our awestruck family and friends in London. It would be mostly valleys and coastline, with a few mountains in the middle we thought. Simple.

While regretting the size of our route planner, when I compare our map book companion to the options available in the twenty-first century, it did have decided advantages. For instance, it couldn't demand that we 'perform a U-turn as soon as possible', if we intentionally went past the suggested turning, without informing our electronic guide that we had changed our route, because we liked the look of the old church in front of us. Nor did we find ourselves encouraged in ever-strident, and often mispronounced terms, to 'turn left at the next intersection', despite the obvious existence of a large and very full harbour in that direction – something the app-based map guides have been known to do, in less well-trodden areas. While we would occasionally lose our way in those days, there were several instances when becoming lost, or stopping randomly, would lead to unplanned but happy outcomes, and it was all part of the adventure anyway.

The third of our essential planning acquisitions was designed to keep us going, whatever our yet-to-be purchased bikes threw at us along the way. The *Readers Digest Basic Guide for the Maintenance of Bicycles*, 1983 edition, helpfully informed us that, 'a well-cared for bike should last its owner a lifetime'. Well, that sounded like good news, because we only needed them to last for the three-to-five months we thought it would take us to get around Europe. But we were also hoping to be able to sell them once we had finished our trip to recoup some cash. So, I liked the idea that they might 'last … a lifetime'. For that piece of insight, if nothing else, it was worth the £1.50 that we shelled out. Although we did also hope that we would be able to use the book to increase our scant knowledge of what to do if the derailleur detached, chains broke, gears stopped working, brake pads needed replacing, mudguards started rubbing, spokes snapped, tyres punctured, or any number of other accidents that might befall us on the road. Certainly, the photos were very clear, the instructions seemed laudably coherent, and just by reading it we felt much better informed and capable – a view we would have the opportunity to disprove on multiple occasions the following year.

So, now we knew where we were going, where we might be able to rest our weary bodies, and how to maintain our mode of transport along the way. Time to take the plunge and buy the two major and essential pieces of kit for this adventure – our bikes and a tent.

As we started to research bikes, we realised that, while we had both ridden bikes extensively, neither of us had ever bought one. Jenny had started her cycling career on a trusty three-wheeler, working her way through a single-gear dragster, a green Raleigh and finally a drop-handlebar bike as a teenager. I had graduated from my own fire-engine-red three-wheeler, to a much-loved single-gear Raleigh workhorse until, at age thirteen, I was surprised by my parents one Christmas Eve with my first drop-handlebar racing bike. I remember it well, because, despite my extreme excitement, I was momentarily dismayed to see that my younger brother was to be the proud owner of a brand new and iconic Raleigh Chopper, which had the centrally located three-speed hub and imitated a Harley Davidson. I soon realised however, that while those bikes were the epitome of cool for a young boy in 1972, they couldn't achieve the speed of a five-gear racing bike.

As an aside, I was interested to learn that Raleigh's own three-wheeler had been the early inspiration for the Robin Reliant car, of Mr Bean fame. A car that achieved iconic status, although probably not the height of British engineering excellence, or anywhere near the epitome of cool. Meanwhile, back in 1984, we still needed to buy our touring bikes for Europe.

So, we turned to our recently acquired and already well-thumbed Readers Digest bicycle guide, which included a chapter telling us how to select the right bike – apparently you needed to look for more than something with the appropriate number of wheels, gears, brakes, and a saddle. With this by our side, we were ready for action. But the question was, Where to buy it? In this we were fortunate because we knew a long-time cycling enthusiast who was well informed regarding types of bikes and, as importantly, where they could be purchased and how much was reasonable to pay. Armed with all this invaluable information, we set out for Richmond one afternoon to buy two Clements touring bikes, fitted with panniers, with racks front and back, and adjusted to fit our shapes. In 1983, these were state-of-the-art for touring bikes, designed and manufactured by an ex-British Olympic cyclist; although, as they were made of steel and reinforced all-over, they were going to test our fitness and strength.

The guys in the shop were intrigued by our intentions when they discovered that we were planning to ride around Europe for close to four months. Their interest was heightened when they saw that Jenny was one of the budding cycle tourists because, as we found out when we made it to the Continent, females touring on bikes were quite rare in the early eighties. However, before we finally settled on which bikes to buy, they had a few key questions for us.

'How much cycle-touring experience do you have?' – A short conversation.

'Are you planning to carry much gear?' – 'Yes, lots.'

'Are you concerned about punctures, and do you want extra protection?' – 'Yes, definitely.'

And…

'How many gears do you want?' – 'As many as possible, so the ten-gear option for both of us, please.'

They were going to adjust our bikes as a result of this conversation, and we would come back the following week to pick up what would become our new best friends – when they had finished fitting the panniers and racks, mudguards to protect us in wet weather, extra padded seats, at Jenny's request, and puncture protectors inside the walls of the tyres – an absolute lifesaver, as it turned out.

A week later, after work one day, we caught the bus to the bike shop where we parted with what seemed to us a large amount of cash. Then, because this was 1983, a time of miners' strikes in the UK, and sympathetic transport workers' strikes, we couldn't take the tube home and we wanted to break in the bikes anyway – so, we had little choice but to ride them back to Jenny's house in West London. At least for this journey we would be on the left side of the road. So, despite London cabbies and double-decker buses not being the most tolerant road users, when it came to wobbly bike riders on main roads, or showing any sympathy for the jet stream generated when they screamed past us on the dual carriageway, we took our first tentative steps towards getting to know our new machines. We also started the process of breaking in the humans who would, we hoped, propel the bikes around Europe the next year.

That just left the tent, in which we would be sleeping every night. In this I was deferring more to Jenny, who had completed her gold Duke of Edinburgh course and consequently had camped more than me. My family didn't take camping holidays and my only experience was traumatising. I hadn't ventured back into the fields again since that event when, as a young cub scout, I had been literally blown off a Welsh hillside with the rest of my frightened pack.

Although maybe this wasn't totally surprising, because in the UK in the late 1960s, some scouting troops had what might kindly be described as a Darwinian approach. You only had to look at our troop's initiation ceremony when graduating from cubs to scouts. Graduating cubs would line up in the parquet-floored scout hall for the 'crossing over' ceremony. Ropes would be placed on the ground several feet apart, in parallel lines to imitate a river. Each cub would be grabbed by their feet and hands, and swung back and forth until they were released; or thrown, to be caught on the other side by their new scout troop. Needless to say, some of them *weren't* caught and the floor was not quite as forgiving as a real body of water might be. In retrospect I'm surprised any of those young cubs ever came back. Or that their parents, watching on, consented to those same scout masters supervising their children on remote camping trips. It was a different time for sure.

Anyway, back on that Welsh hillside – maybe this was another stage in the scouts' continuous attempts to toughen us up, but you would have thought that pitching four tents in a farmer's sloping hillside field was not the optimal way to break cubs into the joys of camping. Perhaps weather forecasts were less reliable then. I'm not sure what was going through the scout leader's mind, but I know what was going through my ten-year-old mind:

'I don't want to be here.'

'It's dark, very wet and the wind is getting stronger.'

'No, I don't want to chase my tent across the fields, there were large cows when we passed by this morning,'

And…

'That toilet looks every bit as bad as it smells, so I think I'll just hold on for the next few days.'

Apparently, that last decision was unwise and needed serious intervention from a doctor on my return, which, in 1969, predated the use of pharmaceutical 'encouragement'.

But I digress and, with limited camping experience between us, we again turned to one of our recently acquired oracles – the AA book. In addition to advising us not to camp on the side of the road, they reassured us that: 'The tent, that basic item of the camping outfit, needs surprisingly little care considering the rugged service it is expected to give.'

They were right when it came to providing 'rugged service'. It would be our home every night for the next four months and, based on the experiences related by other travellers, it would need to be capable of withstanding occasional strong winds and sometimes torrential rain. In addition, it had to be sufficiently compact to fit onto our bikes for travel. So, we didn't want steel poles then. Also, as Jenny reminded me: 'You don't come in the economy size, so it can't be too compact!'

Harsh, but fair, I thought. If the tent had to accommodate us and four largish panniers, then we needed an inner and outer section. We ended up with a structure that kept us dry in our sleeping quarters, provided a rainproof outer, and a smallish section at the front where we could store our worldly possessions, although we couldn't quite drag our bikes into it on very wet days. Still, that was something we were hoping wouldn't be necessary very often. *Riiight.*

Having made this final, large purchase, we needed to trial it, and so my parents' back lawn was pressed into service. We stopped short of actually camping in the tent, as we were overlooked by at least six houses whose occupants were already wondering whether there had been a 'domestic at No. 47' and that was why a large tent had suddenly sprung up in this suburban garden. It all seemed to work on a balmy autumn morning, and we hoped we would become faster than the sixty minutes it took us to assemble the tent at our first attempt. But hope, as they rightly say, is not a strategy.

With the route, bikes, tent and camping all but sorted, we were able to turn our minds to some other important planning elements that would make this an enjoyable adventure.

Budget was something we had considered and then largely ignored, having decided that we would save as much as we could, then spend as little as possible, for as long as possible, (hence the mode of transport). However, we did need to better understand the costs in various countries, so we could ensure we didn't suddenly run out of cash in some far-flung European town. We had also initially drawn some inspiration from a battered copy of Frommer's classic *Europe on 5 Dollars a Day,* although we did note that version was now at least twenty years old, and prices may have increased. Fortunately, the AA book again proved its value, with useful listings of the expected price by camp site, in current values.

We thought that maybe we could manage to keep our spend to five pounds a day, given sterling was quite strong, especially against the lira. We also knew that we would need cash wherever we went, because this was well before credit cards or e-wallets were an everyday expectation. So, we decided to use American Express traveller's cheques, and we dug out our old money belts from our previous globetrotting. One additional benefit of the traveller's cheques would be that we could use Amex offices in various major cities to receive mail while we were on the road.

This brought us to communications, which at the time were mostly by letter; by postcard (which typically arrived home after you did); or by phone, the latter being quite expensive. So, we had to work out a system where, even though we weren't sure when we would arrive in certain locations, we could receive mail from our parents in Australia and England. Thank heavens then for the Amex offices and the more traditional poste restantes that would hold letters for us. The trick would be to make sure we didn't get there before our letters arrived, or we would never receive them, because we wouldn't be going back that way again any time soon. We had also been introduced to the concept of 'PCV', or *payé chez vous*, in France, by our new friends, the AA. This was essentially a reverse-charge phone call initiated through the operator. It would need a modicum of language skills to be able to talk to the operators and communicate what we wanted and likely some patience from said operators – something the French are obviously well known for! Regardless, we thought we'd give that a try, but we had warned our families not to expect too much in the way of voice communications. That turned out to be prescient.

Hard to believe, when you consider the instant feedback loops that exist for anyone travelling now. Before they have even left the monument, view or restaurant, travellers can post photos and comments to all their friends and family anywhere in the world. We experienced this as parents with grown-up children of our own later in life when they travelled. With our son Nick, when he took off around the world, twice, often to remote places like Patagonia and Tierra del Fuego on a motorbike; or posting worrying videos of events, such as jumping off the bridge at Mostar, in Bosnia. And, more recently with our daughter Katy who, coincidentally, undertook her own much more ambitious cycling trip a few years ago with her husband-to-be: leaving from Birchgrove in Sydney, through Eastern Australia, South-

East Asia, Hong Kong, and then a long loop through Western and Eastern Europe, before finally arriving in Budapest. We were not only able to watch their eight-month progress through a specialised app on their phones, but we could stay in touch through posts on various other social media apps. We even knew the day that Dave proposed to Katy, on an island off the south coast of Italy, and watched the drone footage online. We'd still be waiting for the postcard back in the day.

Language was going to be important as well, especially if we wanted to converse with those French phone operators, and it would become a challenge when we moved out of the major towns. We had the pocket European phrasebook but it seemed that, based on my questionable, secondary school French language skills from seven years previous, I was to be the interpreter in France. Phrases such as, *'Où est le toilette?'*, *'Combien est'il?'* and *'Quelle heure est'il?'*, would need to be supplemented by more complex linguistic capabilities.

However, after chatting to a few friends who spoke French very well, my initial doubts receded, and this started to seem like a reasonable plan. Courtesy of the young French lady who taught us at grammar school during our formative adolescent years, my fellow schoolboys and I had been taught the importance of *la prononciation correcte.* So, through dumb luck and the close attention I paid to our teacher for several years (largely due to rampant teenage hormones on my part), my French accent was apparently quite good, when I could get the grammar or words right that is. This would be useful, because the French, of course, are very particular about the way words are pronounced – even more so back in the 1980s when US influence was being actively resisted en masse. So, my task would be to learn as many words as I could that might be valuable in our context, and to refresh myself on the grammar and tenses. And, maybe as importantly, gain a mastery of the Gallic shrug, pause and pout – each of which could be invaluable to enable a native French speaker to put us both out of our misery and interject with the right word or phrase, so that conversation could continue. Sounded like fun and I was up for it.

In Italy, if no English was available, it would be necessary to either find someone who spoke French, which was possible in a country bordering France; use our phrasebook; or we would rely on Jenny. It wasn't that she spoke any Italian, but she was olive-skinned, looked slightly Italian, and had the equivalent of a masters in hand-and-arm waving as part of her usual method of emphasis when speaking. She had been known to accidentally divert entire streets of cars while telling a story at the side of the road, so she was going to be a natural in Italy. And, if in doubt, we'd just point her at the nearest Italian man and she would almost certainly be able to charm him into helping us – so we hoped there would be no problem there.

Switzerland and the Netherlands would be easier, as many people in the major cities that we would be visiting would likely speak English. Which left Germany. Again, a high preponderance of English speakers, but Jenny was going to be the interpreter there, as she had learnt German at school. She did eventually teach me a few phrases – '*Entschuldigung bitte*' was my favourite. But apparently when I said it, I sounded aggressive and a little too much like Colonel Klink from *Hogan's Heroes*, and she was worried that I would alarm shoppers or the average pedestrian. So, I was mostly banned from conversing in German – ironic, because I was continually mistaken around Europe for a Northern German, with my sandy hair and big frame.

Weather was something we weren't too worried about, especially the sun, given Jenny had grown up in the sunburnt country and I had spent a year there acclimatising recently. In fact, although we thought the Mediterranean would be hot, we were more than ready for some serious sunshine after eighteen months back in the UK. Of course, there was a fundamental difference between the two of us, when exposed to the sun. Jenny would sit in the sun for half an hour and come back in looking like she had just spent three weeks on a boat in the Greek Islands. I, on the other hand, possessed generations of British genes that had virtually never seen the sun (apart from time in Oz), and, after spending an entire day in the sun, would move through different shades of white to red – from a passable imitation of a red-topped milk bottle, through to the gold-topped version, with a random sprinkling of freckles for effect. I basically resembled a sun-starved New Romantic who spent too much time in nightclubs, but without the puffy shirt. I would regularly apply the highest factor sunscreen available in the UK at the time, which I recall was maybe SPF8. Whereas Jenny, like many Aussies of her vintage, would liberally apply baby oil so that, as she said, 'I can tan faster.' I guess 'Slip, Slop, Slap' hadn't quite achieved the penetration of today's Cancer Council campaigns. Our planning for rain amounted to throwing in a couple of rain jackets and making sure the tent was waterproof. After all, we were heading for Europe and it was always sunny there, wasn't it?

As for entertainment – for two people brought up in the TV culture of the 1970s in the UK and Oz, and well-adjusted to the pub, club and rugby cultures in London of the early 1980s, we would be taking the equivalent of a social detox. Thankfully we had each other for company – though it turns out that riding a bike for 80 kilometres in a day, over hills and sometimes mountains, generates a strong desire … for sleep, and is a pretty solid passion killer. (Note to self: in future build in more no-bike riding days.) Fortunately, we are both sociable and were eagerly looking forward to meeting locals and other young people making a tour around Europe. Also, we had anticipated the need for some alternative entertainment options and, as well as books that could be swapped along the way, we had invested in a JW Spear's *Travel Scrabble* set. It was amazing what they had squeezed into a small pouch – a foldable, six-inch Scrabble board, one-hundred miniature magnetic letters, four letter holders and a set of rules, in the event of any disputes. We were sure there wouldn't be any, although given our combined strong competitive instincts, it was better to be prepared. Scrabble is a serious business after all.

There was also music for entertainment, and this was the era of the Walkman cassette player, so we were both going to be carrying one of those handily compact 1980s icons, with a couple of cassettes for our time on beaches. Unlike today, when any song, at any time, in any place can easily be retrieved through the abundant streaming services, we would need to rely on our memories while cycling, for songs of significance. That would actually be much safer as we wouldn't be distracted while riding, or in our own musical cocoons. It also wouldn't be difficult because, for most of our generation, music had been a significant presence and influence on the way we thought, behaved, dressed and spoke. It would be hard to understate its importance, given we'd grown up during the musical revolution of the sixties, and then as full and enthusiastic participants in the seventies and early eighties. Although the downside for me was that, for almost every situation there would be a song association, which could easily become a very annoying and persistent musical earworm – starting with Queen's 'Bicycle Race' song, which was certainly better than the other single they chose to partner with that cycle-oriented classic.

So finally, after all these acquisitions and associated planning, we felt we were as organised as we either needed or wanted to be. The trick then was to get our bodies and minds in the right place.

CHAPTER 2
Training our bodies *and* minds for the trip

We thought our bodies might take longer to train than we had allowed, especially as we were going into the colder months in England, when riding a bike with ice and frost on the ground would be less attractive than cadging lifts with family and friends. We did put some bursts in though – again, largely courtesy of the train and bus strikes. Our regular training run was a roughly twelve-mile return ride to work in Central London, with Jenny's house in Stamford Brook as the start and finish. It was an interesting ride then, when the taxis weren't trying to cut you off going past the BBC at Shepherd's Bush, or round Hyde Park Corner on our route past 'Buck House'. Jenny almost lost more than her balance one day, when a black cab spotted a prospective passenger and tried to go through her to snare them as Jenny was turning into Constitution Hill. And we'd heard *Italy's* roads were going to be tough … good training though, we thought.

My other training runs were to and from a few regular haunts – Jenny's house to mine in Harrow; the rugby club for training; and the pub where I was working, to earn more cash for our trip. I won't name the pub, as I wouldn't want to defame anyone, though in a suburb with five good pubs in close proximity, it was locally famous for several reasons. The landlord was an archetypal British publican, a lovely bloke and everyone's friend. His wife on the other hand, was classically unsuited to her role as a publican's wife and was well known for throwing people out from her 'throne' in the corner of the bar – because she thought they had slighted her or made a joke that she considered to be a little off-colour. In England in the 1980s that was just about every joke I heard from my spot behind the bar. Apart from the danger of being thrown out for no apparent reason, it was also known to be one of the safest places in the area to drink – being directly opposite the police station, from where members of the local constabulary would pop in now and again, to 'check things were okay'.

So, while not the type of training that would equip us for the Tour de France, we were feeling quietly confident that our bodies were starting to get comfortable in the saddle.

Turning to our minds, while Jenny and I had both ventured into Europe for very short breaks, we were still relative European novices, so we thought it wouldn't hurt to soak up some context regarding the countries before we set off to visit them. With no internet back then, we were restricted to seeking insights from reading and the various news shows of the day, although they did have a classic British slant. One example of that bias, while possibly apocryphal, still revealed the British media's attitude to Europe. On a day when fog shrouded the main waterway between the UK and Europe, one supposed 'newspaper' headline read: 'Fog in Channel; Continent cut off.' Contrary to this somewhat tongue-in-cheek perspective, which humorously portrayed Britain as the mainland, we were hoping to make Europe the centre of our existence for the next three to four months.

We recognised, of course, that the political climate at that time in the UK might shape Europe's views of the British and possibly us, by association. The UK was going through well-documented modernisation pains in 1983 – largely courtesy of a sharp lurch to the right in politics, as the Thatcher government took on the recently unchallenged might of the unions. It was obvious, even to those of us without a deep interest in politics, that the country was splitting along ideological lines and that, if you made your living digging coal, making cars, or building ships, then the writing was unfortunately on the wall. The Tories also brought a Eurosceptic bias, certainly in relation to monetary union and perceived intervention by the European Economic Community, the EEC, which was causing some angst in Europe towards Britain. Thanks heavens we had an Aussie on the team, I thought, in case there was too much anti-British feeling.

If that was the vibe in the UK, we wondered what we could expect in the European countries where we would be touring, and whether any macro events there would impact our ability to travel through them the following year. We assumed the Continent would be distracted by Euro 1984, the European Football Championship, which would be playing in France while we were touring, but as far as we could tell there was also political and other change afoot over there.

France and Italy both seemed to be embracing generational change. France with their enthusiastic support of a national march by second generation immigrants, who were highlighting endemic racism and pursuing citizenship rights and equality.

While next door, Italy had just welcomed its first socialist prime minister since the Second World War and had also removed Catholicism as the state religion – a massive shift. Germany, meanwhile, was being thrust back in time through the Hitler Diaries hoax, but there were still no pointers towards the enormous changes that would bring down the Berlin Wall six years later. We couldn't really tell what was happening of note in Switzerland, which remained famously neutral on many issues. But the Netherlands was continuing to push boundaries in areas that were often taboo in other countries – in this instance, regulating euthanasia by doctors. Additionally, we knew that our last stop on the Continent was still the only place where you could legally buy mushrooms that would alter your mind, as well as spruce up your pasta dish.

Interesting though this context was, none of these political events seemed likely to inhibit our travelling plans or change our route. The real genesis for the trip was a strong desire to immerse ourselves in culturally and historically significant cities such as Paris, Rome, Florence, Venice, Amsterdam; to explore villages, food and vineyards; and experience the rich art scene available, as we toured through centuries of history and empires. Without the immediate information sources that we now take for granted, we were relatively unaware of what was really happening in those countries, it was going to be a journey of discovery and adventure.

This was part of the appeal for me because I had always been drawn to journeys and adventure in my reading, as a young boy devouring Rudyard Kipling's tales, through to one of my favourite books in the early eighties – *Quest for Adventure* by Everest conqueror, Chris Bonington. I was transfixed daily as I took the tube to and from work, with the exploits of the adventurers in it who conquered oceans, mountains, deserts, continents and more, utilising all manner of transport. If you enjoy true adventure, I heartily recommend reading it. It features many brave individuals doing extraordinary things. Clearly, those adventures involved a much higher level of risk and danger than we were going to experience – unlike Jenny's grandfather in his First World War biplanes, or even my grandfather in the trenches below him. However, those intrepid souls in Bonington's book did provide inspiration and a desire to try something different, and embrace change. And our journey, while not likely to result in physical harm, would at some level, as Bonington says in describing his book, 'involve a journey, or sustained endeavour, in which there are the elements of risk and of the unknown, which have to be overcome by the physical skills of the individual'.

Okay … so we wouldn't be scrambling up the side of a mountain; tramping through blizzards and across ice floes; or making our way over vast, empty oceans on flimsy vessels – but you have to start somewhere, and this would be a significant step-up from our pre-trip, sedentary office-based jobs. In addition, there was less chance of dying, which had to be a positive. We also didn't know of anyone else from our circle of friends and acquaintances who had attempted this sort of European trip, nor were there any reference works we could follow. So, for two young adults from suburban London and Sydney, it offered the adventure we were both seeking.

There we were at twenty-three and twenty-four respectively, with eighteen months' worth of relationship under our belts, and we were both thinking – this would be a bloody big test for us, both physically and mentally. We were effectively going 'off-grid' with only each other for regular company and, if we could manage the challenges thrown up by this trip, then it would be quite an achievement, and maybe proof that our relationship was something special. We were also pretty fit and used to exercise from a very young age, having played competitive sport – Jenny played netball, skied, was a good runner and swam well; I had played competitive tennis and rugby and also ran a lot. We both enjoyed the outdoors, we were used to cycling by now, and we were very adaptable and excited at the idea of spending many months exploring those countries. We were confident in our planning, but also wanted to allow enough freedom to change plans as and when the mood or other factors dictated. We were ready to go. Time to organise some boozy farewells and pack.

Ah yes – packing … and unpacking … and re-packing. It did appear that we had a few more belongings between us than four panniers could reasonably accommodate. We had also decided that we were not going to have backpacks, as it would make it harder to cycle, so it was time to start reducing. We had moved back into my parents' house at this stage before leaving for Europe. Jenny and I both have a clear memory of my dad coming into our room to see how things were going – as context, he ran his own removal and storage business for forty-plus years and so was well practised in assessing spaces and what would, or would not, fit. He didn't need to say anything. He just laughed, shook his head, and went downstairs to make himself a cup of tea. He later told me that he thought we had about twice what could sensibly fit into those panniers, laid out on the bed. In the end, because the excess seemed to be more Jenny's than mine, she offered to make the final calls on what did and didn't make it, so I retired for a cuppa as well. So … that was how the very red, and very high-heeled shoes made it into *my* panniers.

Now, we were ready to go.

CHAPTER 3
Getting started: London to Lyon

And we were off. It was late April 1984, and we were thankful for my dad's help to drive us to Victoria station nice and early. This saved us lugging all our gear, except for our bikes which had already been consigned and which we would meet again in Lyon – we hoped in one piece. Maybe the difficulty of carrying our gear without bikes should have warned us for the other end, but we were excited and both extremely optimistic people, so we didn't give it a second thought.

As our designated ferry to Dieppe sailed out of Newhaven, I was a little nervous. Not for the cycling trip, but because I had been well known to suffer from travel sickness. As a youngster on our annual holiday trips to Cornwall, I often didn't make it to the end of our road before my dad had to stop the car, for me to remind everyone what we had for breakfast that day. I needn't have worried as it turned out, because on this early spring day, we had a very calm sea – which was just as well, because those old ferries had no stabilisers and would often rock back and forth like a baby's cradle, with a predictable reaction from most of the passengers. I don't remember much about the crossing, but I do recall meeting an English lady around my mum's age who had sons in Australia – prescient maybe? We also attended a Brownies' tea party, at Jenny's insistence: 'To help them earn their badges,' she told me.

I was happy to help and figured it couldn't hurt to rack up a few 'brownie points' for myself, which I would undoubtedly need over the next few months. There certainly were a lot of earnest young girls, decked out in the uniform that gave them their name. Many with sleeves covered in badges describing their achievements, including music, first aid and camping – the last of which brought back cub scout memories for me that I'd just as soon not recall. I presumed this event would earn them their tea-making badge, in addition to raising funds for a charity for underprivileged children. A good cause all round and a very welcome cup of afternoon tea accompanied by home-made tea cakes. I couldn't think of a more English way to say farewell to England for a few months.

Then we were in Paris … one of my favourite walking cities in all the world. Although Paris could be an intimidating place for the British and Australians. For some reason, when confronted with the average Parisian, we would just go to water. Maybe it's because we assumed that, while our French was basic at best and often non-existent, every Parisian we met could speak fluent English but was choosing not to do so because … well, because they were Parisians. So, we were very grateful that Jenny had a friend in Paris – one of those young Parisian women for whom entire lines of traffic would stop so they could watch her walk across in front of them. She was also mostly unaware of the impact she had on others, being a lovely, generous person. She was to be our guide and interpreter for the next day or so and the first order was to head straight for the Café de la Paix. Because as she said in her accented English: 'It's one of Paris' most famous eateries and you 'ave to eat there.'

Now that was more like it. Refreshed and impressed, I then did my human-mule impression with the panniers and tent, as we trekked halfway across Paris to an apartment, owned by her friend's parents, for a shower and dinner.

This was a treat and slightly unusual. First, we were eating dinner at 10 pm – a time when most British and Australian families were safely tucked up in bed; and second, we were also being treated to French home cooking – quiche, veal and a rich sauce, accompanied by her parents' vintage French wine. Don't get me wrong, we ate very well at home. But you can't really compare the 1980s standard British fare of meat and two (extremely well boiled) veg, or fish fingers and mash, with the delights of French cuisine. Also, the British Sunday lunch treat of a slightly warm bottle of Black Tower, Mateus Rosé or Blue Nun, didn't really compare to genuine *vin de France*. Those friends also went some way towards disproving my jaundiced English view of all Parisians, by generously giving me my first opportunity to trot out my schoolboy French. While everyone spoke good English, they agreed to talk in French and were patiently helping with colloquial phrases and pronunciations. Like any English schoolboy learning French, I had already become familiar with various French expletives, the mildest of which was *merde* – a term that was often pressed into service in the UK. However, some of the more everyday local and non-insulting phrases they were teaching me would be useful as well. It also allowed me to further observe and practice my own version of the Gallic pout and shrug, until we pulled the pin just after midnight. I went to bed silently thanking my French teacher. A full day, but a very positive start. The next day would be sightseeing and as I've declared already, other than London, I don't think there are many better cities in the world than Paris in which to indulge that passion.

'Bugger, that's frustrating,' I said when I heard the news the next morning.

It seemed the train drivers of London had been chatting with their French counterparts and the TGV trains would be on strike the following day for our trip south. We hadn't realised in our research that the French were upset about Thatcher's mining closures as well – although after a few months on the Continent, we would come to realise that the French transport workers in the 1980s had never known a strike in which they didn't want to participate. Luckily there was a slow train we could take instead, so we would be able to catch up with our bikes. Though being a French public holiday – of which there appeared to be many – we'd be sharing it with holiday-makers, so it would be crowded, and we were sure they'd appreciate us loading all our bags and panniers on when we boarded

This brings me to one of the many paradoxes that I've observed, associated with the French. On the one hand, to give the French some credit, having always personally been a big supporter of public holidays and work-life balance, I did and still do admire their continual dedication to deriving joy and happiness from life, or their *joie de vivre*. However, I think maybe I was also starting to understand the more earnest British government's reluctance to 'go all in' on the EEC, especially monetary union. Being in economic partnership with the French in 1984 would have been like entering into business with that very entertaining and slightly glamorous friend, who took long liquid lunches daily, was constantly taking sickies, and had ten weeks annual leave – great for them and fun to be with, but one-way traffic in terms of inputs and benefits. The good news for us was that we were more interested in experiencing and sharing in the French capacity for relaxing and having a good time while we were touring, so the economic consequences of their attitudes were less important to us.

Thankfully, when it came to finding new train tickets, Jen's French friend helped us negotiate the practised rudeness of the French ticket office 'customer service officers' – an oxymoron if ever there was one. Now we were organised and able to catch the train the following day, so we could head off for some sightseeing. We had been to Paris before but hadn't seen Notre Dame cathedral, which was perched on the Île de la Cité like a miniature castle on an oval birthday cake. So, we headed straight there. It was a very hot day, which is the only explanation I can think of for what happened next. As we were approaching the cathedral, Jen's friend announced, 'I'm 'ot and I need to make a quick change.'

So, without further ado, she handed me her backpack, popped into a handy ancient stone doorway, partially unzipped the front of her jumpsuit, and promptly unhooked and took off her bra.

'Hey,' I called out, catching Jenny's attention.

'Paris *is* clearly as liberated as most English people think it is!'

Her friend, seemingly unfazed by this pit stop, grabbed her backpack, stowed the clearly excess clothing, and carried on chatting to Jenny as if this was the most natural thing in the world.

The heat was clearly having an effect on more than just Jenny's friend, because later that same afternoon, I was sitting in a secluded spot, lost in my thoughts, when Jenny said, 'I think we need to find a ladies' toilet … and fast!'

Unfortunately, over the years, Jenny would have similar experiences in major capital cities around the world. I think it's an unusual and under-reported allergy to major global cities. But she tells me it's more likely due to swallowing a quantity of varnish as a two-year-old, and the subsequent stomach pumping that has made her occasionally sensitive and nauseous after rich and exotic foods – France should be fun for her then, I thought at the time. Unfortunately, I couldn't really be of much help, so as Jenny and her friend traipsed off, I made myself comfortable with our recently purchased local bread and cheese. I had started to feel French already – though the can of Coke resting beside me would give me away to any self-respecting Parisian.

Once they returned, it became clear that Jenny was feeling too poorly to continue any sightseeing, so we walked back to our hotel and settled her into our room to sleep off the nausea. Her friend and I then headed out to find some groceries that would tide Jen and me over the public holiday. Of course, we bought these in Galeries Lafayette – where else? It was a pretty upmarket department store that sold all manner of posh and expensive goods, but it had a food section and was a serious upgrade from our local Sainsburys in Harrow. Jenny and I ended our day snacking in the hotel room while trying, and failing, to decipher a French TV game show. To be fair, I'm not sure that was just a language issue – most game shows I have ever watched can be initially indecipherable, unless you are one of their avid fans, and this one did look particularly pointless. Still, all in all, it had been an eventful first full day on the Continent.

We were looking forward to being reunited with our bikes and had a relatively uneventful trip to Lyon, where they were waiting with only a few recently acquired scratches. That was a relief and, after checking them out and loading up our panniers and tent, we grabbed a local map from the information centre and set off purposefully. We then took a wrong turn and proceeded to get hopelessly lost in very hilly terrain. I'm not sure where the promised valleys and rolling hills were, but clearly not in this part of Lyon – I was thinking that when I got back, I would have a word with Messrs Collins about their map book. We eventually discovered the correct route, found the town where our camp site was located, got lost again, and finally rolled into our camp site in Dardilly, five hours after leaving the train station. Not quite on target for a supposed ninety-minute trip.

We learnt two important things on our first day cycling – Jenny knew how to read maps and compass directions and I knew how to read street signs. Obviously, the former was going to be more valuable than the latter for most of the trip. But, in my defence, as I said to Jenny, 'I've never needed to read a compass.'

You couldn't see the sun in London most days to work out which way was north anyway, and the public transport and cabs were so abundant that you were never likely to get lost. On the good news front, we got the tent up fast, the camping gear worked, and we decided to stay for a few days while Jenny recovered her strength from her illness and our challenging first-day ride. It was time to crash.

CHAPTER 4
Our *Route de vin*

Most people with an interest in France and its geography have heard of the Rhône River Valley, which flows all the way from the Swiss Alps to the Mediterranean. However, it was the section that runs south from Lyon which interested us on this trip. A part of the valley that had been conquered, influenced, and subsequently settled by many peoples – the Celts, waves of Mediterraneans, and the Romans. As a result of those diverse and longstanding influences, it had plenty of towns and castles that appeared to have sprung fully formed from your favourite chocolate box cover. Along with more recent nineteenth and twentieth-century influences, which had delivered bustling centres of industry and commerce, new tourist attractions and, of course, wineries. In fact, it was probably best known for the wineries, hence the title, *Route de vin.*

Our plan was to follow the Route Nationale 86 all the way down to Avignon, along the Rhône River Valley, with occasional forays along the legendary Route Nationale 7 when necessary. The RN7, or *La Nationale Sept*, was well known because it had been the escape route to the south for generations of French families from the 1960s onwards. It had been called many colloquial names, including *La Route des vacances*, winding as it did from Lyon all the way to the French and Italian Rivieras – it was basically the Gallic equivalent of Route 66 in the US, but with good food and wine. Part of the attraction for the French people was likely the fact that they could climb into their family Renaults or Citroëns and drive slowly (always wise to drive *those* cars slowly) through some of the best wine country in France, while resting at Michelin-starred restaurants and roadside cafes, which served gastronomic delights to weary travellers along the way. The trip to and from their eventual destination was said to be as much a part of the holiday as the time on the Riviera – you do have to admire the French for their dedication to continual research into food and wine.

But back to the N86, which ran alongside RN7 for some way. We chose it as our main road south because, while it was originally built to link Lyon with Nimes, it mirrored our desired route almost perfectly and would be mostly free of large trucks – unlike the larger RN7. It was also rumoured to be 250 kilometres of splendidly picturesque road, winding through fields of poppies; past spectacular sloping vineyards, which clung to steeply rising cliffs; and often going straight through medieval towns that were surprisingly intact. Unfortunately, you can't find it on a map if you go looking for it now. The road has been transferred, in a bureaucratic exercise, from 'National' to 'Department' level. So, it now goes through five different 'D' roads and parts of the original route from Lyon have been absorbed by motorways. The route south is poorer for it, in my opinion, and shows a surprising departure for the French, from their usual dogged reluctance to abandon romantic associations with the past – which the old N86 surely had. In 1984, however, the N86 was still very much intact, and was prominently signposted the whole way as the *Route de vin* – a good sign and we were quite happy about it.

We had invested in a *Guide Michelin,* so we could now make sense of the roads and, more importantly, see where the contours of the hills meant taking a smaller side road for a short distance would be prudent. Progress indeed. Since that first day's ride, we had spent several days north of Lyon, ostensibly checking over our bikes and camping gear to make sure they were in working order, and girding our loins for the journey south. We also started our diligent research into the local *fromage*, *vin*, *pain et pâté*, as well as kicking off the French leg of our Scrabble championship. All very critical to soak up the French way of life, we thought, although it became interesting when we started allowing occasional French words in Scrabble play – I'm not sure what JW Spears would make of that, or whether we had enough letters to cope with this trend when we reached Germany.

One thing we had known for certain during our planning phase, was that that our language skills would be tested as we progressed. We didn't expect that would happen quite so early, but we did end up in two of our more bizarre, but charming, encounters during our ride south from Dardilly on that first day in May.

Our initial experience was when a young Frenchman staggered over and accosted us, while we were resting at a cafe and drinking lemonade on a warm spring day, en route to our next camp site in Condrieu. He'd spotted our heavily laden bikes and it had apparently struck a chord. He told us: 'I made a similar trip a few years ago.' And even though it was only mid-afternoon, he continued: 'Let me buy you both a drink, *s'il vous plaît.*'

'*Merci, vous êtes très gentil*,' I replied in my halting French, because that was indeed, very kind of him. Although that afternoon, he did have a distinctly alcoholic aroma, which suggested he may have been celebrating continuously since that momentous event. But, not wanting to appear rude, we graciously allowed him to buy each of us a glass of wine and then left quickly before things could deteriorate. He seemed happy enough as he waved us off – at least I think he was waving to us.

Later that day, as I was wandering near our camp site in Condrieu, looking for a *tabac*, I again found myself unexpectedly in a long conversation with a local. This time with a man who must have been seventy-plus and whose lined, sun-tanned face and work-worn hands hinted at a life spent mostly in the fields of his native Provence. I was struggling with his strong accent, and he was clearly not following my halting French, but we eventually found common ground. We were able to reach agreement that Sacha Distel, that well-known French singer from the 1970s, was 'fantastique'. I think he'd gone through Charles Aznavour and even Edith Piaf before we arrived at this conclusion.

We parted in mutual confusion, but not before I'd had the chance to practice the Gallic pause and shrug, which seemed to allow him to insert the words he wanted, and we could carry on conversing.

'I'm getting the hang of this language stuff,' I optimistically declared to Jenny on my return to our tent. So, I was dispatched to find a newspaper from which we could predict the weather for the next week. I found *Le Figaro* and spent a happy half-hour trying to decipher the weather terms, which to be fair, even in your own language are often understood only by mariners, sheep graziers and weather aficionados. I felt I was getting close, when

Jenny helpfully pointed out that I was translating yesterday's weather forecast. Still, if history was a predictor of the future, we could expect quite a lot of wind and rain.

We were also starting to familiarise ourselves with our tent and camping for real. When we were practising the assembly of the tent in my parents' backyard, we were quietly confident that we would be fine. What we hadn't experienced there though, was the hard, rocky ground, which we found along the banks of the Rhône. After several futile attempts to assemble the tent in Condrieu, a German cycle tourist took pity on us, lent us his mallet, and gave us a few large pegs to help us keep the corners of our tent down in the wind. Ah yes, the wind. It seems that a tent makes various noises in a strong wind that mimic someone breaking into a tent, as it tears at the zips and guy ropes. I was dragged from a deep sleep on one of our early nights in Condrieu by this very sound and I must have been convinced, as I found myself standing outside our tent with a torch and my Swiss Army knife – ready to defend our Anglo-Aussie honour.

On the positive side, our gastronomic research was continuing and Condrieu was also justifiably famous for its white wines. Although on our budget, the stuff we were drinking, while being a nice Côtes-du-Rhône and an improvement on Blue Nun, was unlikely to make many sommeliers' playlists. The food, however, was another matter. We had been told that the food could vary considerably by region, so we were determined to ensure that we did the appropriate amount of research as we moved along the Rhône. In this town we tried their local cheese, the Rigotte de Condrieu, a tasty goat cheese, which we accompanied with foie gras, spicy sausage and fresh bread to restore our energy. To add to this gourmet banquet, Jenny whipped up a wonderful tuna pasta dish with a local sauce, cooked on one gas ring in the howling wind – no mean feat. As cycle tourists it was probably best that we went easy on the wine anyway.

The next day it looked like the 'forecast' from *Le Figaro* was going to be right and the rain was coming from everywhere. There would be no riding in that. Our tent was holding up well and we only had to make the occasional dash to the toilets between Scrabble sets, and to refill our water for tea. We weren't quite expecting what we found in the closest and most convenient toilet block though – as European novices, our first experience of squat toilets. Uh-oh … I was flashing back to that Welsh hillside as a cub scout in 1969 and their questionable conveniences, though being older and more mature I persevered this time.

'Clearly the average Frenchman doesn't eat a lot of curry or drink much Guinness,' I told Jenny confidently, 'or those squat toilets would have been retired many years ago!' I was thinking that they wouldn't have lasted long in London or Sydney, that was for sure.

We also had our first experience of French phone operators, and it went pretty much as I had expected. I talked for a little while, trying to explain that I wanted to place a PCV call to the UK. They then showed the sort of patience for which telephone customer service representatives are famous – they talked quickly, shouted a bit for effect, asked me to repeat myself and then, with an exasperated sigh, hung up. I'm sure they felt much better once they had worked out that I was one of those notorious *rosbifs* – *merde*! So, I tried again with the same results and then paid thirteen whole francs, which was more than one quarter of our daily allowance, for a call to let my parents know we were still alive and well. Mind you, we should cut the French some slack – after all, a failure to understand, or to demonstrate patience for foreigners speaking a different language was hardly just a French problem. Anyone who had witnessed a Londoner speaking agonisingly slowly and in a very loud voice to any poor tourist who stopped them to ask for directions, would agree that communicating in a foreign language was a universal challenge for tourists everywhere.

On the next day the rain stopped, and we were off south, to Tournon. The wind was showing the same changeable nature as the previous day's phone operators, but it had swung around behind us, for which we were very grateful. It was a 51 kilometre trip, and the countryside could sometimes take our breath away as we rounded a corner to see the fields stretching away to the mountains on both sides of the road. It all looked very familiar to someone who had seen plenty of French countryside populated by lone cyclists in wartime movies, when the plucky Allied airmen were trying to escape the clutches of the Nazis. I know this is a classic caricature, but war movies and TV series set in that time were very popular in the UK in the seventies and eighties, and, as I've mentioned before, the British do have a certain attitude towards the French. I think the TV show *'Allo 'Allo!* had a lot to answer for. In fact, if I had seen an old man cycling towards me on his battered bike, dressed in a blue-striped shirt, beret on his head and onions around his neck (like the 'Onion Johnnies' who used to pedal around Britain), I wouldn't have been at all surprised.

But back to our ride. We were able to cover it in under five hours, so we decided to stop in Tournon, set up the tent, and see if we could find a place to eat a meal in a local restaurant.

We wandered into town and were drawn to the castle, which had provided quite diverse services since construction in the sixteenth century – from the residence of aristocrats, progressing through to its time as a prison during the French Revolution. There was a certain cyclical nature to that, given the aristocrats were the main target of the revolutionary forces. I wouldn't have been surprised to discover that some of the pre-Revolution inhabitants had ended up being accommodated in their previous home, but under quite different house rules – and with fewer servants. The castle was now an innocent-looking tourist attraction and there was a classically French restaurant in its shadow. Feeling flush, we wandered in, ordered a four-course meal with a local Chablis, and finished with what we took to be a creamy cheese. It turned out to be a local delicacy, which was a mixture of cottage cheese and cream – my fault as the interpreter apparently. Nevertheless, in the spirit of trying local delicacies, we gulped it down as best we could, paid the bill and strolled back to our tent, feeling pleased with our first foray into the regional restaurant scene by ourselves.

The following day was the second public holiday in two weeks. Good for the French, who, as I've said before, certainly knew how to live. We had grand plans for a long leg south, but it was a public holiday and if we saw an open shop we typically stopped to take advantage. Especially when it was in a town of such medieval charm as Guilherand. Most of what we had been admiring as we rolled slowly through the town was from the thirteenth century and was built around an old Catholic church, which was still there. Although the town was much older and had been continuously occupied since prehistoric times – becoming firmly established after Caesar who, knowing a thing or two about *properly* occupying a country, settled some of his veterans there during the Gallo-Roman era.

Jenny was just emerging with her haul of fresh fruit and staples from a little roadside *tabac*, where we had randomly paused our ride, when she was stopped by a middle-aged lady who had followed her out of the shop. She was blonde and had the casual elegance that French women often seemed to effortlessly project and, as she chatted to Jenny, she proceeded to ask, in near-perfect English, 'Would you like to join me and my family for lunch? Then adding, as if we needed an incentive, 'Our house is just around the corner.'

We assumed that she had looked at our shopping and taken pity on us, but it was a very generous offer and of course, we jumped at it.

'Mai oui, bien sûr, et merci beaucoup!' I replied.

It did turn out that she was also keen for us to meet her daughter, who was a similar age to us and learning English. Either way, we weren't protesting. The terrace where we were to eat was in the grounds of their stunning thirteenth-century house, which had originally been a hostelry for pilgrims travelling south and who were, as Jenny eloquently summarised in her best faux Strine later that night: '… following some religious bloke.'

This banquet was an upgrade from our plans, which would have been a picnic at the side of the road with crackers, cheese and fruit. Our hosts, Bernard and Michelle, had set up lunch, with their daughter Sylvie, accompanied by two very affectionate Labradors, and plied us with five courses and accompanying wines. I wish I could describe the courses and wines in more detail, but things did start to blur after a while, unused as we were to drinking in the middle of the day. We stayed for four hours, chatting about our trip, our families, the town, France, and all manner of topics and could easily have stayed until dinner, if we hadn't known we needed to find a camp site.

When we finally wrenched ourselves away from their hospitality, with promises to visit if we were back, we headed off down the road like Tour de France veterans – propelled by the food and especially the wine. We hadn't gone far when I had to shout to catch Jenny's attention: 'Why's your back tyre starting to look like a deflated balloon at a kids' birthday party?'

Damn, our first puncture of the trip. At least we had ridden out of sight of our erstwhile hosts. Fortunately, it was a relatively minor puncture. Once we had patched it up and chatted to a touring Dutch cyclist, who had stopped to offer helpful advice, we decided to camp at the first opportunity, which was a lovely little village called Beauchastel. Only 10 kilometres on from our new French friends, it was a very well laid out camp site on the banks of the Rhône, but much to Jen's disgust, with only squat toilets again. I was wondering if I should tell her we were going to have to get used to that. We didn't need much food after our lunchtime banquet, but we convinced ourselves that it was necessary to sample the local baguette and pâté, accompanied by homegrown and home-made apricot jam, from the lovely family with whom we had passed much of the day. Well, Europe in 1984 had some great things going for it already – we wouldn't have experienced that spontaneous French hospitality if we had been slavishly following a twenty-first century Ms Google. It seems looking up and over the handlebars, rather than continually looking down at the phone, has its value.

It would be fair to say that our recovery the day after our impromptu French food and wine feast was slow. Not altogether a bad thing, given the wet French spring was continuing. We did manage to rustle up some pasta and a local *piat d'or*, which didn't compare to either the food or vintages of the previous day, but for eleven francs, which was less than one pound sterling, we couldn't really complain. It oiled the wheels of a PCV conversation later that day, which ended in a similar manner to my previous attempts – but where this time, the French operators and I were able to exchange our respective views on their customer service ethic, and I was able to outline improvements that could be made. I think they took it rather well, though it was hard to tell over the loud noise the phone made when disconnected from their end. We ended the day with a haircut *pour moi*, by Jenny – she said it looked good when she'd finished, even though she was using the small scissors on our Swiss Army knife. We didn't have a large mirror to check, so unless people started pointing and laughing when we continued our journey south, I was inclined to believe her.

We were in a nice camp site though, so we spent a day lazing in the sun and the next day we woke to *le vent qui rend fou* – the wind that drives you mad. *Le Mistral* had arrived. This was definitely not a gentle breeze, but something that sped in like a steam engine at full throttle, roaring down the Rhône Valley at speeds of up to 90 kilometres per hour. It had been known to blow the people of Provence and their possessions away. Despite this considerable inconvenience, those same people were perversely fond of their wind. It brought benefits that shaped the excellence of their wine region – blowing away the clouds to leave bright, sunny days in which the grapes could ripen, and drying those same vines after rain, of which there appeared to be plenty.

With the sound of this gale-force wind tugging at our tent the next day, we took a while to convince ourselves there was a better place to be than inside our sleeping bags. On the positive side, when we did eventually rouse ourselves and climb onto our bikes, the wind was travelling in the same direction as us – south. So long as the roads didn't turn in an easterly or westerly direction, we would be fine, we thought. But the bridge at Montélimar does exactly that and, as we turned east to cross the river, we were literally pinned to the railings on our bikes and forced to dismount and walk them over the long and fully exposed expanse. I took the walk twice because the wind became so strong that Jenny couldn't force her bike across, even after she dismounted, so we needed my extra weight to manage it.

There was some compensation, however, because the route was taking us through many beautiful parts of the country, which were well worth a visit. We stopped briefly in the twelfth and thirteenth century villages of Châteauneuf-du-Rhône and then Viviers, to admire some of the medieval streets and châteaux, which appeared well maintained. We weren't well versed enough in the wines of France at the time to know that the former makes some of the most impressive red wines in the country. That was probably a good thing, because they tended to come with equally impressive price tags.

While we had only been cycling for about ten days, we had been taking our transport for granted, apart from the early puncture. That changed as we were exiting the winding streets of Châteauneuf-du-Rhône, when Jenny's chain decided to disengage itself from the derailleur. Maybe it was the challenge of the constant gear changes as we rode up and down the hills and streets in the elevated old towns. Inconvenient and a bit messy though it was, it was easily fixed. At Viviers, however, we had a more unexpected bike challenge. As Jenny was riding along the road, just after we'd stopped to buy some Montélimar nougat, the entire luggage rack and panniers slid off the back of her bike. She took it very well, but this posed a more difficult problem, given it was the fault of a snapped bracket.

'Do you think the extra weight from the large blocks of nougat pushed your pannier over the edge?' I asked, innocently. 'I did offer to carry them on my bike,' I reminded her.

Once she had finished good-naturedly treating my observations with the contempt they clearly deserved, we managed to improvise by tying a considerable amount of string around the frame and rack. We then limped the last 24 kilometres to the camp site at Bourg-Saint-Andéol.

It was another twelfth century town and this time we were following in the footsteps of French luminaries such as Victor Hugo, and allegedly, D'Artagnan and his musketeer compatriots – though I'm guessing they didn't stay in our camp site. It was certainly a lovely old medieval town. On a more mundane note, almost nowhere was open for food, as we had miscalculated the date of the previous public holiday. We finally stumbled across a pâtisserie that was just closing, but prepared to sell us some bread and cake, for a large sum of money. Still, we figured if it was good enough for Marie Antoinette, then it would be good enough for us.

We continued our journey south and to get to Avignon, we needed to flip from the smaller and pleasant N86, to the larger and considerably busier RN7. The good news was that the wind was behind us all the way to Orange. However, we were also buffeted by trucks and their slipstreams on the larger road, which made for a few hairy moments. Fortunately, the makeshift string 'bracket' on Jenny's panniers held and, after we turned onto a smaller road for the last few kilometres, we coasted into our camp site on the Île de la Barthelasse. This place was well laid out, even though it was very exposed to *Le Mistral*, being in the middle of the two Rhône tributaries. The AA had recommended it as: 'a very pleasant site, with tall trees and well-marked … on hard standing ground'. But we'd also been told that that it was flood-prone and could be marshy, hence the absence of development. Well, there clearly hadn't been any floods for quite some time, because the terrain was rock hard and we struggled to get the pegs into the ground again, even with our newly acquired mallet. We ended up borrowing some large stones from the riverbank to weight the pegs and tent ropes down, to protect our tent against the not-so-tender attentions of the wind. Clearly, I hadn't quite been able to shake that windy Welsh hillside cub scout experience.

If you ever visit Avignon and find yourself camping, the location on that island was the drawcard, with its picture-perfect views of the Pont d'Avignon – the song about which had been an annoying and constant earworm for me ever since we set off on the road that morning:

Sur le Pont d'Avignon,
L'on y danse, l'on y danse,
Sur le Pont d'Avignon,
L'on y danse tout en rond.

Apologies if I've just done the same thing for you. There was contention regarding the song though, with many people believing it was composed in the sixteenth century, some time before the collapse of the bridge in the seventeenth century.

'Maybe all the dancing laid the seeds of destruction?' I wondered out loud to Jenny.

On closer examination, it seemed that the original dancing in the song was not actually *sur* or *on* the bridge, rather, it was *sous* or *under* the bridge – and it actually took place on the Île de la Barthelasse, where we were camping. It was apparently well known during that earlier time as a place for enthusiastic partying and music in the many open bars scattered around the island. It was only in modern times that *sous* became *sur* in the song. In reality, the bridge had only been wide enough for a cart to pass anyway when it operated before the collapse, and so would not have been somewhere for the Avignonese to dance the farandole, or any other popular French jig of the period – so it wasn't the dancing that caused the collapse then.

Avignon deserved a longer stay and, in addition, we needed to find a bike shop that would be able to repair Jenny's wounded machine. So, we booked into our camp site for a few more days. One of which, the tenth of May, would turn out to be a very auspicious day for us, two years hence – the groundwork for which, we like to think, we laid on this adventure – but more of that later. In 1984, we were more interested in exploring the old town, finding a bike shop, and continuing our exploration of the local food and wine. A bike shop proved a little harder to locate than we had imagined. But finally, after finding an establishment where the cost of repair quoted was less than the original cost of the bike, they were very good about fixing it quickly. It also became apparent that the French took cycling and touring very seriously, and the bike mechanics were extremely interested in our trip, our route and again, the fact that one of us was female – and an Aussie.

With both bikes fully restored, we were now able to confidently explore the town, and we found to our delight that Avignon had some impressive and well-preserved UNESCO World Heritage Sites – well, the Palais des Papes was well preserved. Obviously, the Pont Saint-Bénézet (or Pont d'Avignon), was less complete, though what was left was well cared for. The town itself was still surrounded by 5 kilometres of robust stone walls and several sixteenth and seventeenth century houses graced the old town. It had been settled more than 5,000 years before and, like many Rhône Valley towns, had moved through Gallic and Roman occupation.

The town of Avignon was both famous and infamous for the period in the fourteenth to the fifteenth century when it operated as the site of the popes during the great schism in the Catholic Church. Famous, because of the palace and the influence the French popes commanded at that time, but equally infamous, for the way in which they both acquired that influence and then used it to subjugate the populace. Shocking for a dominant religion in the Middle Ages to take advantage of their flock, I know, but there it is.

The culinary and wine experiences in Avignon were a little more challenging and unexpected. First, our traditional lunch of a local camembert cheese, pâté and bread looked inviting as we spread it out on the ground to eat. However, we soon realised that *Le Mistral* was also attempting to spread it out – across Avignon. So, we were forced to take turns to hold down the food while each of us ate our fill. Next, I was amused to see the labelling on the mincemeat we had bought for dinner that night. It declared in small print that it was *pour les animaux* – I was wondering how to break it to Jenny that it was intended for pets, which we did not yet possess, rather than our dinner plate. And finally, when we returned late to our tent, we found that a small animal had decided to feast at our expense, and the brand-new camembert in our bag was almost completely consumed. It had left the garlic sausage alone, which to be fair had been our choice too, after sampling it the day before. Consoling ourselves with alcohol, we then discovered that the French do sell bad wine to one another, not merely the English – our bottle of *blanc de blanc* from the Intermarché supermarket could comfortably have stripped paint and was not one of our finest purchases. But then, for the equivalent of only fifty pence, that was hardly surprising.

The following day, as we were cycling back to our little island, having again explored the town, I was reflecting on another confusing communications' interaction – because we had decided that we were going to be more effective with aerograms, given the PCV challenges to date. And, having been sent into the local post office to buy a supply of those handy letters for the trip, I had left the premises wondering whether my old nemeses, the French phone operators, were working in the post office on their days off, after I was shunted between four different counters for this relatively simple purchase. So, slightly distracted by this experience, as we rode out of Avignon, I wasn't paying complete attention to the traffic flow. I was dragged from my reverie by the honking of multiple car horns as we attempted to navigate the circular road exiting the old town – we did wonder momentarily if we had wandered onto the film set of a grand prix movie, as the cars sped past us in seemingly random directions.

'Maybe *Le Mistral* really *is* the wind that sends people mad,'

I called out to Jenny, as I executed another swerve to avoid a car turning left across my front wheel. The drivers had certainly become more erratic as we headed south.

Despite this apparent increase in risk to life and limb, from the motorists with whom we were sharing our trip, that was not the major influence over our discussion later that night and our decision to reconsider the route once we hit the Riviera. Rather a more in-depth look at the topography between Marseille and Cannes, courtesy of our Michelin guides, and also a judgement by Jenny that: 'There are better beaches further along the coast.'

I wasn't sure that any self-respecting Sydneysider was going to admit there were better beaches anywhere else in the world, so the bar was high for her comparisons, but she did have a point. It looked like we would avail ourselves of the train system after all, once we reached Marseille, for some of the south coast, bypassing a section of the route that was likely to have fewer inviting beaches and also looked quite mountainous.

CHAPTER 5
The French Riviera: Marseille to Menton

We'd been in France for about three weeks and, as we moved through the wine districts and small towns in the Rhône Valley, we were starting to feel more acclimatised to the French way of life. Unfortunately we didn't need to acclimatise to the weather yet, as it had followed us all the way from London. However, as an Englishman, I had been taking longer to settle into the French rhythm than Jenny. I think this was mainly because I had been bombarded from an early age with the English bias that France's culture and way of life were more frivolous, less productive, and somehow not as 'worthy' as the English way of living. And, almost re-enforcing that stereotype, it was true that in 1984, the French attitude towards customer service in many professions could be characterised as 'the customer is mostly wrong' – contrary to the English and the Australian cultures, which were more likely to err on the side of the customer. I know it sounds like a cliché, but those who had the 'pleasure' of an encounter with a French telephone operator, bank teller, post office clerk, gendarme, ticket collector, or general government bureaucrat in that time, will tell you that I may even be understating the situation.

But, and it is a big and important *but*, when we took the time and attempted to speak the French language; introduced ourselves properly according to local customs; and engaged in a positive manner, the French we met could be wonderfully warm and exhibited the *joie de vivre* for which they were justly famed. On our short trip to date, we already had plenty of positive examples – such as the very kind family in Guilherand, who invited two perfect strangers to a long and sumptuous lunch; the many local artisan bakers and pâtisserie owners, for whom their profession, and their customers' enjoyment of their product, was obviously a passion; and the camp-site owners and small winemakers, who took the trouble to explain, to a couple of obviously poor travellers, the secrets of their town and local wines. We had decided that we liked France – we liked the French way of life, and we especially liked their food and wine – and we would be sorry to leave her when the time came.

In the meantime, we were still in France and transitioning to a different region. As we headed south again from Avignon, we were leaving the relatively flat sanctuary of the river valley and, according to our maps, things were about to become challenging for anyone on pedal-powered transport. On the bright side, we were moving into the allegedly sunnier climes of the South of France. We were also passing sign after sign proclaiming that Salon-de-Provence was the town of Nostradamus – no point phoning ahead then, as they undoubtedly knew we were coming already. Although maybe we took the wrong route, because we didn't see a welcoming committee when we stopped on the other side of the town for a quick picnic lunch. It turned out to be very quick because we only had the garlic sausage left, which had even been rejected by the animal in our tent back in Avignon. It was a real 'smeller', and we couldn't manage more than one bite each – clearly, we hadn't completely acclimatised on the culinary front yet.

The road did in fact become difficult quickly when we cleared the relatively benign valley, as we expected, and we had to ascend two small mountains in quick succession to reach our destination. Then we experienced shades of our questionable Lyon navigation skills on our first cycling day, because we overshot our intended camp site in Vitrolle, just to the north-west of Marseille – which doesn't reflect well on the AA's directions, incidentally. So, we doubled back and still ended up at a different site. At least this time, *I* couldn't claim the 'credit' for misreading map directions and finally my London-honed street sign expertise came in handy, allowing us to follow the signposts to this new camp site. It was clearly going to be around the larger cities, like Lyon and Marseille, where small and large roads intersected, that it would become more challenging for cycle tourists. Still, we covered 80 kilometres in six hours, which was pretty good riding that early in the trip, although we were both sore by the end of the day.

'Yesss! Finally, a glorious day of blue skies and sunshine,' Jenny called out.

You could tell who the beach bunny was. Okay then, shorts and thongs (to use the Aussie vernacular) would be the order of the day – although in the South of France in the 1980s, the French version of a thong wouldn't have been out of place on the beach either. In addition, we'd do a short bike ride without panniers to buy supplies from a village that was chosen because it was *not* in the hills. However, we had forgotten about the early- to mid-afternoon French tradition of a siesta. Very convenient for the locals because it meant the shops were open later in the evening and the busy shopkeepers could go home and have a snooze – but for young travellers who were very hungry at 1pm, not quite so convenient. Oh well, it gave me a chance to try to even the score with a few games of Scrabble in the sunshine while we waited.

We had also started to notice a few differences as we reached the South of France. This camp site was the first time we had been asked to pay for a warm shower, but it wouldn't be the last. Also, the accent had changed. It made sense that France, as well as the UK, had regional accents; it's just that we had never considered it until then. I guess to our untrained ears all of the accents in the regions sounded the same. I must say though, the southern French 'yes', which sounded to us much more like 'away' than '*oui* ', had been throwing us a little. That was until we realised they were not asking us to 'go away', rather they were agreeing with us. Tricky stuff this language comprehension.

The next day, I was back in the office of the camp-site owner, who was apologising for the unseasonable weather – very decent of him I thought.

'*Une autre nuit s'il vous plaît,*' was all I could say in reply.

It was sounding a little like a broken record to both of us, I expect. Another night at the camp site and the weather was starting to feel familiar to an Englishman – the skies opened at 8 am and kept raining on and off until 9 pm, so we weren't going anywhere. I had also noticed that, southern French accent notwithstanding, the language was becoming easier. This was fortunate because most of our conversations with authorities and camp-site owners were in French now, as the incidence of English speakers decreased noticeably as we headed south. I think the camp-site owner probably also felt sorry for us, because he donated a couple of cans of spicy sardines for our dinner. He did offer some tinned escargot as well, but with all of the rain, we were seeing more than enough of those little creatures crawling up the outside of our tent, and we weren't acclimatising to the point where we wanted to try any of those particular local delicacies.

Well at least I didn't need to ask him for another night the next day. He knew that, from the look on my face, when I sprinted into his office between the rain squalls that had been coming in waves through the previous night and into the next morning. The following day was still quite suspect, but I couldn't face asking for another night, so we packed and pedalled off. Unfortunately, the road quickly became mountainous between Vitrolle and our destination in Aubagne, on the other side of Marseille. And, while it may seem that we were constantly complaining about the climbs that kept popping up on our route, it's worth bearing in mind that we had decided to travel by bike so we could afford to stay on the Continent for longer. Not because we had a longstanding desire to test ourselves against the mountainous landscape of the south-west corner of the French Riviera. We were also there for the weather and unfortunately, the rain was not cooperating. So, we were convinced that shipping our bikes on to Cannes and then catching up with them by train, a few days later, was the smart plan.

Of course, once we'd decided we didn't need to ride the next day, out came the sun. So, taking advantage, we wheeled our bikes into the train station, to consign them to Cannes, where we left them on the train platform, worryingly leaning against the wall in the public area, but with assurances from the ticket collector that they would reach their eventual destination. Placing our trust in the French train service, we marched off towards the town square, where we managed to stumble into a wine tasting event – which is better than stumbling *out* of one, I guess. We found a vintner who spoke very good English, and he could describe the qualities of each of his wines in detail and in a manner which we could understand. We were relieved and grateful and, to do justice to his enthusiasm, we gallantly tried all six of his wines … several times.

'Finally, quality wine that we can afford!' I whispered to Jen.

Armed with our bottle of Viognier, which only cost us twelve francs, we walked the 5 kilometres back to the camp site to one of Jenny's magnificent culinary creations – pork, with tomato and French-inspired onion sauce – still on one gas ring. We weren't sure if that was the recommended 'pairing' for our wine, but it worked for our relatively immature palates!

Since arriving in France, we had been trying our best to adapt to the laissez faire attitude of the French and leaving things to take their own course – with varying degrees of success. For an Englishman brought up on order and predictability, this had its fair share of challenges; though Jenny was making a much better fist of it. This may be because in Australia they have a saying – 'She'll be right' – which as far as I could tell when I was there in 1982, meant something very similar in spirit to laissez faire. Fortunately, that adaptation to the French way of thinking was to prove helpful the following day. When we turned up to meet the camp-site manager at the appointed time, with our bags, tent and gear for our promised lift to the train station, we realised that he had either forgotten or, more likely, it had been lost in translation the day before. No matter. He quickly pressed one of his long-suffering and long-term tenants into service, and the poor fellow had to fit all our bags and the two of us into the back of the family Citroën, with his two wide-eyed, and hopefully not traumatised, children on their way to school.

Later, as we sat contentedly on our relatively short train trip to Toulon, and then on to Cannes, I was smiling more and more and thinking we had made a good decision, as we sped easily through one set of mountains after another on our way to the French Riviera proper. When we arrived and walked out onto the main street, everyone seemed to be more smartly turned out than we had expected in the middle of the day, causing me to turn to Jenny and say, 'I think we might be a little under-dressed!?'

It was, in fact, the week of the Cannes Film Festival, which has been a regular feature for the international film business since the 1940s – and why wouldn't you take a paid trip to Cannes if you were in that industry? Unfortunately, we just didn't have enough pressed white linen in our crumpled bags of clothes to make the grade on the promenade. We did slowly walk along the front with our bikes in any case, hoping to see some of the stars of films being premiered, such as *Another Country*, which featured a young Rupert Everett and Colin Firth. There were certainly many young and beautiful people pointedly posing on the waterfront, in the hope of being discovered – but we had lesser hopes, given that we were pushing a couple of touring bikes and were decidedly not dressed for the event. If only we'd been given a bit more notice.

Without the prospect of a very large Hollywood contract to keep us in Cannes, we hopped onto our bikes and made off towards our destination for the night – Villeneuve-Loubet Plage. We didn't know much about it, but we liked the sound of the name, and it had the French word for 'beach' in the title, so that seemed good to us. The ride took us up and down the coastal headlands, but the views made the ascents worthwhile, and we pedalled through familiar sounding towns, such as Juan-les-Pins. This town in particular sparked another musical earworm for me, which was annoyingly on continual loop – Peter Sarstedt's 'Where Do You Go to My Lovely'. The song is about a young woman who grew up in Naples and found her way to the upper echelons of French society, and as he relevantly sings, for her summer vacation, she goes to Juan-les-Pins. As someone who had always loved ballads with interesting stories, I remembered the song well. To be honest though, it was very distracting looking for the style of swimsuits he also references, as we were cycling through the millionaires' playgrounds of Cap d'Antibes and Juan-les-Pins.

When we arrived at our camp site, we quickly discovered that Villeneuve-Loubet Plage was famous for several reasons. The founder of *Le Guide Culinaire* and *haute cuisine* was born and lived there in the nineteenth century, which clearly in France was very important and maybe a good sign? More infamously, Marshal Pétain lived there from the 1920s – someone who had been hailed as the hero of Verdun after that calamitous campaign during the First World War but then made a spectacular error of judgement when he founded the Vichy state to collaborate with the Nazis in World War Two.

We had reached one of the places on the Riviera where the luxurious yachts and motor cruisers reputedly came to supplement their crews with cheap, young travellers, before heading off for more exotic parts. Although, while the thunder and lightning continued, we weren't going to be seeing much action there. So, as soon as there was a break in nature's light show, I was dispatched to the massive *supermarché*, which made the larger grocers back home seem like local corner shops. I was only looking for some milk and Swiss milk chocolate – the satisfying and occasional breakfast combination we had convinced our twenty-three and twenty-four year-old selves was providing just the right balance of dairy and energy. As well as being very tasty, it had been demonstrated to be healthy in moderate amounts – although probably not the one kilo bars we were consuming before our rides. Still, when you were fit, in your early twenties, and riding 50 to 80 kilometres most days, you could easily work that off. What was amazing to me when I entered that warehouse-like structure, was the volume and breadth of goods being sold under one roof. In England and Australia, that scale of enterprise just didn't exist in one store. If my shopping aspirations had been more expansive, and if I had possessed the funds, I could easily have left my shopping trip with a new bike, or even a windsurfer, in addition to our daily breakfast needs.

The next day we rode back to Cannes for a closer look and as we cruised through the Côte d'Azur, we stopped in Antibes to have a stroll round. It was an interesting mix of old and new. You could still walk through the old sixteenth century town, which was dissected by streets running in all directions and surrounded by mostly intact ramparts. Just below the old town were scores of magnificent and relatively new mansions looking down on the now virtually empty marina, where we assumed the beautiful boats and luxury yachts usually crowded for mooring space, if they weren't all on their way to more exotic places for the summer. It certainly achieved an almost effortless chic, in the way that many French towns seemed to have monopolised.

We thought we might be a little late to connect with boats seeking their summer crews, looking at the empty berths in the marina, but we asked around anyway. We found an English marine carpenter who was working the coastline for the summer and who confirmed our suspicions.

'If you'd been here four weeks ago, the boats were queueing up to hire young crews to sail to Tunisia, Morocco and the Mediterranean ports,' he told us.

Oh well. That might have been interesting, but as I said to Jenny, as we walked away, 'I'm not sure the owners of those boats would have appreciated me sharing the contents of their daily menus over the side on a regular basis!'

Continuing on our bike ride was probably a better option, on balance.

Despite this small disappointment, this was still the place to start getting serious about some 'bennys' as Jenny called them – or beneficial rays of the sun. Not a term you would hear now, given what we know about the sun's rays and consequent skin damage. But this was still 1984 and if you were on the Côte d'Azur, you were going to head for the beach to tan the body beautiful. And that was exactly what we did, to a beach called Plage de la Garoupe, where there were a few surprises in store for us. As context, my own limited experience of beaches growing up in the UK had been mostly in Cornwall and Devon, and the beaches there could be beautiful – framed by sand dunes and soaring cliffs, like a Turner classic. But the idea of going into the water without a drysuit on those beaches, was about as appealing as standing in your local butcher's cold store, and with roughly the same result. However, I had also enjoyed the recent privilege of lounging on some of Australia's stunning and vast beaches, as had Jenny of course from an early age.

For both of us then, we were surprised to find that whenever and wherever we sat down on this or other beaches, a family would almost certainly come and place their towels in close proximity. In Australia this would draw looks of disdain and pointed comments from your average beachgoer. We also hadn't been prepared to find large parts of beaches, such as this one, roped off and with a user-pay approach. Again, a state of affairs that would have escalated quickly in Oz, probably to questions in parliament, so fundamental a right was free public access to beaches. Maybe that's the egalitarian nature of the Australians. Although it may also be that in 1984, only a little over fifteen million people lived across that vast land, so there was always an empty beach you could claim for yourselves with a little effort.

Back on that French beach, we did manage to find a small space to claim for our sun-worshipping, without an attendant family as company. Then, when satisfied, we trotted back to the promenade behind our beach, to discover our first brush with thieves and loss of essential kit – some passing stranger had clearly been very thirsty and helped themselves to our water bottles, from both bikes. They wouldn't be expensive to replace, but it was a reminder that not everyone would be as well-meaning and well-intentioned as those we had met in smaller inland towns to date. Welcome to the Riviera.

'It looks like I'll be going back to that supermarket tomorrow, to find replacements,' I said to Jenny. 'I'm sure they'll be just behind the windsurfer aisle.'

We had heard that Nice, often mentioned in the same breath as Cannes, was very … pleasant, to avoid the obvious pun. However, before we arrived there we had to climb up and up on our bikes, until we were riding around the cliffs, along spectacular winding roads, and through tunnels carved out of the rock. With the scenery and the constant glimpses of the sparkling Côte d'Azur, I started to understand why the James Bond franchise had kept coming back to those roads again and again. The famous Aston Martin had roared around those same bends and through Juan-les-Pins, Cannes and Nice over the years. We were certainly taking a slower, less glamorous means of transport, and possibly seeing more as a result. But I was thinking it would be good to come back at some stage, when we had money, and hire a soft-top sports car to drive through those roads and towns. It's always important to have a dream.

When we reached Nice, we were a little surprised to find the expected sandy expanse bore a startling resemblance to the pebbly Brighton beach, back in the south-eastern corner of the UK, but without the pier. Mind you, the water looked a damn sight more inviting in Nice. Not only was the sea a stunning shade of turquoise, but it didn't look like you would need to cover yourself in grease to spend more than sixty minutes swimming in it, as you would have to in the English Channel, off Brighton.

The Nice beach also had quite a connection to England, with the 7-kilometre Promenade des Anglais curving its majestic path along the seafront – an avenue that was built to remember the English aristocracy, who apparently developed a penchant for spending their vacations in Nice at that time. The English aristocracy in the nineteenth century had made an art form of not doing very much and they were well known in European circles for spending chunks of their inherited wealth as they did so, wherever they went. Nice was also competing at the time with cities like Venice for aristocratic sponsorship on their European tours, so this was probably a pragmatic and commercially smart act on the part of the merchants in Nice. Frankly, given the long and often bloody history between the English and the French during the nineteenth century, it was all quite surprising to find the English honoured in that way, but I guess money has always motivated the well-off burghers of seaside towns.

We had been busy admiring the beauty of the French Riviera and enjoying the positive aspects of the French at play. So, it was only natural that we would be brought back to earth by the bureaucrats from the Amex office, who, after Jenny had queued for nearly two hours, wouldn't tell her whether there was any mail for me.

'Looks like those France Télécom customer service reps are also moonlighting in the Amex office in Nice!' Jenny said, as she stomped out.

We decided to press on to Monaco. That soft-topped Aston would certainly have come in handy on those mountainous roads, but we had to make do with the low gear ranges on our bikes. It was a spectacular view as we coasted down into the port. Although, when we finally reached Monaco – a port that was filled with very expensive-looking boats – our eyes were drawn to the steep mountain on the other side, which we knew we would have to climb to leave the town and continue our journey. Monaco was an interesting place on many levels. It was scenically beautiful, it had impressive infrastructure, and it was one of the richest places on the planet. In fact, it still is. Largely courtesy of the complete absence of income or capital gains tax for established residents – essentially anyone who lives there for more than six months in a year.

They also benefit from the Monte Carlo Casino – queue another musical earworm for me, this time courtesy of Peter O'Toole in *Lawrence of Arabia*, with his rendition of 'The Man Who Broke the Bank at Monte Carlo', sung in the Arabian canyons while travelling by camel to meet Prince Feisal. Okay, it's not the obvious place to hear that song about the Monte Carlo Casino, but it's still a bloody good movie. It seems the world's most well-known casino was not always the money-making guarantee it was by 1984. It took the vision of the Grimaldi family, which still controls the principality today, to build what we were seeing and importantly, the infrastructure to get people there so they could be parted from their hard-earned. Something for which the residents of Monaco were eternally grateful, we suspected, as it enabled their tax-free existence.

When we made it to the Monte Carlo quarter of Monaco, we realised that this was a place designed for people with conspicuous wealth. That didn't describe us in any way, so we thought we'd better find the Amex office to check for mail, before continuing through the built-up area. We had reached the top of that enormous hill and I stopped to ask directions from the doorman of the hotel, which sat astride the peak. He seemed a little amused, but graciously pointed us in the right direction to the Amex office.

As I re-joined my laughing cycling partner, she pointed behind me and asked, 'Did you see that sign declaring this is the site of the famous Monte Carlo Casino?'

I glanced back over my shoulder to where I had just received directions, and saw the casino, from which the same doorman was happily waving at us.

'Oh well,' I replied

'I'm guessing he knew we weren't coming in!'

And, in any case, not only had we forgotten to pack Jenny's cocktail outfit and my black tie, but there were inexplicably no bicycle racks for our customer demographic.

We were now at our last camp site, in Menton, before leaving France. And, despite our overall appreciation for most things French, they weren't quite finished throwing curve balls at us yet.

First, none of the banks would change francs to lire on the French side of the border – imagine needing lire when you get into Italy?

Next, we found that Michelin expected you to travel into Italy before you could buy more detailed maps of the countryside there. Obviously no need to plan a route until you are actually riding on it.

Then, the French Télécom operators seemed to be on industrial action – all ten of the phone boxes we tried were giving us an engaged tone for PCV calls.

And finally, the French weather gods didn't want us to leave – they threw in a little thunder, lightning and torrential rain to emphasise the point.

On that last note, even the locals were bemused by the weather patterns we had been experiencing during this European spring.

We were expecting more sunshine, but this felt like a typical English spring to us.

However, Jenny's encounter with a well-known French amphibian was the pick of the tour so far and the coup de grâce. She had disappeared to the sole shower cubicle, halfway up a hill, to indulge herself with a nice hot shower. When she returned to the tent, she laughingly described her new shower routine to me. It went something like:

Start hot water timer.

Avoid hopping amphibian.

Grab available waste basket.

Cover still hopping amphibian with basket.

Keep one foot on basket to keep amphibian from escaping.

Soap and wash self, while standing on one leg.

Finish shower and dry self, still on one leg.

Decide whether to release or cook amphibian.

Fortunately, Jenny has a forgiving nature and a good sense of humour. So, when she'd finished describing her shower companion, and I had finished laughing and failing to be empathetic, we decided that releasing it back into the wild would be best. We weren't really sure how to prepare frogs legs anyway and we had our eyes on a pâtisserie we had passed earlier in town, where we wanted to walk, to rest our bike-weary muscles.

When we arrived there, even though it was a Sunday, the place was jumping with strolling families, the restaurants were full, and the pâtisseries were busy. It would be our last day in France for a while, so we treated ourselves and bought two very large cream cakes – to be consumed while engaging in the time-honoured tradition of people-watching, which we happily did on the main promenade in Menton. A perfect way to spend our time as we drew towards the end of our last full day on the French Riviera.

Reflecting on the time that we had lived and travelled among our hosts for the last month, that proximity had created, in both of us, especially this Englishman, a greater appreciation for the French and their way of life – which was sort of the point of the trip. It had also become less obvious to me why the French and English invested so much apparent energy into maligning one another. Clearly there were differences in the way the French and English generally approached life, and it had become a national sport for both country's media to regularly have a dig at one another – doing no harm to their circulation when they did. Also, the sense of humour of the English (and Aussies for that matter) was very different to the French – I was not sure that the average French person would realise that, when an English native 'took the piss' (to use the vernacular) with an insult, it was often a backhanded compliment. Similar to the Aussies, if they liked you, then they typically insulted you to your face. Although given it was mostly with a deadpan expression, that could be understandably difficult to discern, if you weren't from one of those two countries.

There was also some considerable historical basis for the residual enmity between the French and English. For a start, the two countries had spent almost nine hundred years fighting one another. The list was long and even a short summary demonstrated the point – from the invasion of England by the Normans in 1066; through the Hundred Years War in the Middle Ages; hostilities during the Napoleonic Wars; and colonial tensions in Canada, America, and parts of Africa through the eighteenth and nineteenth centuries. Even as far afield as Australia, one wonders what might have happened if Lapérouse had arrived before the First Fleet landed in 1788, rather than several days afterwards. Maybe the Aussies would have been singing *La Marseillaise* and drinking predominantly French wine, instead of exporting their own wine to outsell the French in the UK. Then, in the twentieth century, when the English and French finally found themselves on the same side, in two horrific world wars, the English couldn't quite escape the suspicion that the French resented them for having to rely on that support and active engagement for their eventual liberation.

So, with different approaches to life, sense of humour, the historical enmity, and the back-and-forth one-upmanship by the respective media to keep it current, it was perhaps not surprising that this uneasy relationship existed. Maybe, I thought, the reason was not so complicated, even if neither side of the famous Channel readily wanted to admit it – the British and French were family. It may have been a distant and even estranged branch, but it did, and still does, show all the signs of family squabbles, albeit occasionally bloodier. The more recent Brexit histrionics demonstrate that, where the British unexpectedly spat the European dummy and where the shocked French have been at the forefront of exit negotiations. They have been eerily like a messy divorce – Who pays whom maintenance? What about access rights? and, 'How do we stay on civil terms when we continue to live in the same neighbourhood?'

To the English, the French may have seemed like the annoying uncle, who appeared at the Christmas dinner with his new, glamorous wife and fashionably dressed children, and who went on to cause squirming discomfort for their more conservative hosts, as they animatedly discussed their latest holidays on the Riviera. To the French, the English may have seemed like the boring cousins at the party, who kept talking about the weather, the superiority of their football league, the 1966 World Cup; and who all appeared to have been dressed by 'Marks and Sparks' or Debenhams. Both characterisations were clearly exaggerated, although with all the other cultural and historical differences, it's little wonder that the English and French often disagreed. But, as with most 'families', they knew deep down that they needed one another. And, for what it's worth, my reflection in 1984 as an Englishman who had spent a little more time among the French, was that despite the differences and mostly media-driven enmity, Britain and France should be doing all they could to preserve that familial relationship and support.

That seemed like a good note on which to retire for a long night's sleep and finally, having spent the previous evening relaxing and reflecting on the French leg of our journey, when we woke, we were ready for the next chapter of our adventure. We could see Italy from there, literally on the other side of the port and we were raring to go on a beautiful, sunny spring day – the weather gods had finally deigned to smile on us.

'*Allons-y*! and *Andiamo*!' I called out to Jenny, as we cycled towards our next country.

CHAPTER 6
Easing into Italy, the Italian Riviera and the mountains

We had the easiest transition imaginable across the border – the customs officials took one look at us and waved us through, without even stopping us. I'm guessing they figured they could easily catch us if they needed to question us further, as we slowly cycled 100 metres past the checkpoint and then stopped to take our photos, as proof of crossing into Italy. We were thrilled to be in Italy, which rejoiced in the nickname of *Bel paese*, or beautiful country. Our impressions from afar and from meeting Italians through our travels were that, if the French loved life, the Italians took that to another level – hugging it tightly, in a continual passionate embrace. We were looking forward to experiencing that celebration of what the Italians liked to call *La dolce vita* – the sweet life. In fact, there was one Italian phrase that had always resonated for me: '*Mangia bene, ridi spesso, ama molto*,' 'Eat well, laugh often, love much.'

In our valiant attempts to understand and embrace the Italian culture while there, we were more than prepared to give that a go.

As we moved into Italy, we noticed a worrying early development – when looking into the places where we might camp, there were only twenty-six pages of entries in our AA book, versus the seventy pages of camp sites for France. Granted, France is almost twice the size of Italy's land mass, but we were hoping that this difference was more due to the AA running out of steam when they made it to Italy, rather than an absence of places where we would be able to rest our heads.

On a more positive note, the cost of living in Italy looked like it would be cheaper for us than France, and the exchange rate against the pound sterling was very good. Although, I almost didn't benefit as I was hoping. I'd changed my remaining French francs into the princely sum of 85,000 lire after we crossed the border. Somewhat confused with the juggling of currencies, I then changed another one-hundred pounds sterling at a larger bank later in the day. But when I finished counting the cash outside the bank, I realised that they had given me the US dollar rather than sterling exchange rate, and it was quite a difference, in their favour. At that point I had low hopes, but after I girded my loins and went back into the bank, my Italian customer service experience was then a surprise to me. After my time in France, I was expecting to be shuffled from counter to counter in the hope that I would eventually lose either my patience or the will to live, and then leave their premises. Not a bit of it. The teller took one look at the receipt he had given me, apologised for the mistake, and gave me the balance owing without any argument.

'I like Italy already,' I said to Jen, as I emerged from the bank with a relieved smile on my face.

With a developing positive mindset about our Italian hosts, we embarked on our planned route, which had a few hills but was mostly coastal, and an easy ride with the wind behind us – to our first Italian town, San Remo. We arrived in the middle of the day, and this gave us the chance to have a brief look around yet another old medieval town perched up in the hills, with its twelfth century cathedral and thirteenth century houses dotted around the narrow streets. They looked down on a lovely, sheltered seaport, perched at the end of the Liguria region, which in turn stretches in an arc, around the edge of the Mare Ligure. It did all look rather as we expected an Italian town to appear, complete with small groups of older men lounging around outside cafes, many of whom were calling and waving to us good-naturedly as we rode past. We quickly located our camp site, which was 50 metres from the seafront, then headed to the local supermarket to stock up with goodies for dinner. With our arms full of ravioli, Italian bread sticks, ice cream, biscuits, chocolate and more, Jenny remarked, 'Italy's cheap compared to France!' We were getting around 2,300 lire to the pound sterling, and you could buy a lot of gelatos for that.

However, not speaking the language was going to prove a little challenging. While my French had not been anywhere near fluent, we could make ourselves understood with patience on both sides. But, in Italy, we had yet to encounter anyone with sufficient English language for us to speak our mother tongue, so the phrasebook was already getting a solid workout. Jenny's advanced hand-and-arm-waving technique was also truly appreciated here, even if they weren't quite sure what we were saying to accompany the gestures all the time.

The next morning, as we headed into town, we were passed by the third peloton of racing cyclists we'd seen that day.

'Wow, the Italians really seem to love their cycling,' I called out to Jenny, as they charged past us. We had heard it was a national sport in both France and Italy, but we were seeing a lot more cyclists in Italy. I didn't know if this was related to the seventy-fifth anniversary of a famous cycling race from Milan to San Remo, colloquially known as *La Classicissima,* which had finished there a few months earlier in March, or whether this was just normal. Although it wasn't just bikes that were on the roads. After only a few days in Italy, we were forming the view that the populace was obsessed with anything on two wheels – bicycles, motor bikes and scooters.

We lost count of the number of scooters we saw; most of which were predictably either a Piaggio, which was apparently celebrating its one-hundred year anniversary, or a Vespa. The latter interestingly were also manufactured by Piaggio and meant 'wasp' in Italian. And, as we watched one after another of those Vespas weave their way through the traffic, mostly steered by young men, with the obligatory young woman nonchalantly riding side-saddle on the back, with headscarf blowing in the wind, they sounded very much like a swarm of wasps.

Jenny was also being warmly welcomed by the Italians on many levels. As I've mentioned before, she had a slight Italian look to her, which had only increased since spending a month cycling in the (occasional) southern sun. She was also riding a bike, and a touring bike at that, in a cycle-obsessed nation. Italian men being what they mostly were in the 1980s, this was not escaping their attention wherever they were gathered, when she rode past, as one of the few women on a bike. But when we stopped and she started to talk, despite the Italian-like gestures, she was obviously Australian – and the Italians *loved* the Australians.

This was not surprising, given the history of migration from Italy to Australia during the 1950s to the 1970s. It started with waves of migrants trying to escape the dire post-WWII situation in Italy. Then with assisted passage for Italians from the Australian government, as the UK migrant numbers failed to keep pace with the Australian labour growth demands. In all, something like 300,000 Italians had made the one-way journey in that period, settling initially in the suburbs of Sydney and Melbourne, but also working on major regional building projects, such as the Snowy Mountains Hydro-Electric Scheme. This meant there weren't many places in Australia that were untouched by Italian migration, or without some ongoing contact with the 'old country'. So, many Italians still had first-generation family or knew someone in Australia and they were keen to let us, and especially Jenny, know about it.

We also saw evidence of a recent and famous British incursion into this particular town – apparently Queen had been the headline act at the San Remo Musical Festival in February. I expected that, given the cycling-mad nature of the Italians, Queen's 'bicycle song' would have been a major hit with the crowd if they played it – queue another musical earworm for me. Later that evening, as we were lying in our tent finishing off our very cheap and quite good bottle of Frascati, I thought that earworm had become a little more persistent and somewhat louder than usual, until Jenny mentioned she was hearing Queen as well. Not in my head then, but rather coming at high volume from the radio in the tent next door, which was occupied by three young partying Germans. Now, I'm a big fan of Queen, as is Jenny, but by 3 am, we were ready for them to stop singing, and I was deployed to use my only German phrase, with as much force as I could muster – which is quite a lot.

'*Entschuldigung, bitte, meine herren*!' I said.

When I appeared back in the tent Jenny was laughing, because apparently this translates to 'sorry, please, gentlemen' – which in fairness seemed a very polite English way of asking them to shut up. She then told me it probably didn't matter what I had said, because I had said it with such force that I had startled her, let alone the occupants of our tent next door. Either way, it had the desired effect, and we were able to sleep at last.

When we hit the road the next day, a little groggily after our early morning encounter with our German neighbours, we discovered that the road to our destination in Alassio was going to be very hilly. And the view that greeted us when we glanced to our left was certainly encouraging us to keep to the coastal road. Only a short way inland, the mountain ranges seemed to stretch into the distance like a set of breakers rolling onto Manly Beach on a sunny Sydney morning. Even on the relatively less mountainous route that we were taking, the roads did climb up and up as if they would never stop. Given this seemed to be the landscape we could expect for some time, we were persuading ourselves that shortening the daily distances would be a good plan, to preserve our bodies.

I was also making a mental note to write to the AA when we returned to Blighty, in addition to the publisher of our map book. We were struggling to find any AA-nominated camp sites in a few of the towns, having to rely on the signs erected by the sites themselves and the tourist bureaus, where they existed. In addition, I was trying hard not to be a judgemental Brit, as I looked for friendly locals along the route. The older Italians in general would shout encouragingly when they saw us go past, but many of the younger Italians we saw did seem a little too busy posing on their scooters, on their beaches and in their bars, to notice us or return any of our waves. Maybe we just looked too dishevelled and bike-weary for their *elegante* self-images?

When we finally reached Alassio, if we were looking for the 'classically Italian coastal resort', that town seemed like it might qualify. It was a very popular tourist destination, being built around an old port and possessing a 3-kilometre curving beach, which stretched off into the distance. Many of the hotels in the town literally opened onto the sand, although our camp site was in a slightly less prestigious location, with its own private, but very pebbly beach. As we were cycling past the port, it was clearly the time of day when the fishermen gathered, and, somewhat inevitably, Jenny was the subject of the openly ogling attentions and calls of the crusty old *pescatori*, which she had learned to take in her stride by then.

The town was a seaside resort though and we were in Italy, so we felt it important to conduct research into the local gelati – and we had a wonderfully decadent cone with lashings of chocolate *and* After Eight ice cream. This was a pleasant surprise, but would clearly not be an isolated experience, as there seemed to be an almost infinite number of flavours. There would be nothing for it but to sample as many as practical while in Italy, so we could report back to our friends and family in case they found themselves in the vicinity. It seemed that ice creams, or gelati, might become the equivalent of our cheese explorations in France, even though the Italians themselves reputedly produced over 2,500 different varieties of *formaggio*.

Given we were still navigating by our large map book, we went looking for some more detailed maps in town. Unfortunately, we were hampered somewhat by our inability to translate what we wanted effectively, so were still struggling to replicate anything with the detail of our French Michelin guides. Strangely, the postcard I had bought to send to my parents had the most detailed outline of the coastline we had seen to date, so we would likely keep that, until we found something a little more helpful. As I reflect from this vantage point, I realise that's a specific twentieth century image – navigating by a physical map, from something called a postcard, both of which have mostly been replaced by digital versions. I think that is a shame, especially the postcard. It used to be a pleasant surprise to receive one of those typically colourful means of communication, from a family member or friend from some far-flung part of the world, or even somewhere like Brighton.

The next day, because the pebbly beach at our camp site wasn't to our liking, and the sun had well and truly come out to play, we walked round to the main beach. It had an interesting layout for people used to the surf club-oriented Aussie beaches. For a start, about one third of the space was taken up with a combination of wooden changing rooms and showers, at the back of the beach. This differed significantly from the more 'spartan' Australian changing facilities in surf clubs, or the single cold showers stationed at the back of most beaches, to wash off the sand. In addition, a further third of the beach in Alassio was taken up by row upon row of pay-per-use deck chairs. We did also spot some Germans lying on the sand on their towels and, while we were unsure if we would be charged to lie on the beach, we figured there was safety in numbers, and so we plonked our towels down in the same general vicinity. I must confess, without wishing to malign our future German hosts, I did wonder whether they had engaged in the time-honoured tradition for German tourists who find themselves near a body of water and had snuck out before breakfast to claim that part of the beach with their towels.

We spent nearly four hours on that beach and had plenty of time to observe the Italians at play. And, while I didn't want to denigrate the male members of the local community, it was tempting to fall back on classic caricatures, when we were confronted with a passing parade such as the one we were enjoying. Either men of a certain age, with hairy chests, shirts undone to the navel and with medallions swinging as they walked; or heavily groomed, budding Lotharios, with hair gelled to a Travolta-like perfection, who were strutting along the front of the beach – to be fair that didn't work quite as well without the flares, platform shoes and white jacket, but they got significant points for effort. Queue a 'Stayin' Alive' earworm. Jen also observed that it was a little strange for us to hear men conversing animatedly in Italian and then bursting into song unexpectedly, in heavily accented English. On a positive note, though, we were certainly being well entertained that afternoon by the locals, which was very good of them.

It was a hot day, and we were seriously considering our first swim in the Mediterranean. Though we did have in mind the worrying warning that our AA friends had given us in relation to European beaches: 'Tourists should be aware that pollution of the sea water at European coastal resorts, particularly on the shores of the Mediterranean, represents a severe health hazard.' They went on to suggest that: 'Not many popular resorts wish to admit this, but now realise the dangers and erect signs, albeit small ones, forbidding bathing.'

We had been looking for that 'small' sign, *Vietato bagnarsi*, which we understood translated to, 'It is forbidden to get wet', but we had yet to see one. So, either it was all clear, or they didn't really care too much about it. Either way, we needed to cool off in the Med.

This may have seemed like a simple exercise, and to a Sydneysider like Jenny, who had started to swim before she could walk, indeed it was. But to an Englishman who had only learned to swim at the age of twenty-two, when I ventured to Sydney two years previously, I did have to contend with the inescapable fact that my swimming style was a triumph of effort over technique. But then I had been following in the glorious aquatic traditions of many English people of my vintage. In my own case, when presented with a sixpence each week by my mum for my swimming lessons, at the age of twelve, I had decided it would be much better spent watching Tarzan swim croc-infested rivers in Africa at the Saturday morning pictures, rather than tackling the suspiciously *object*-infested waters of our local 'swimming baths'.

In Alassio, we were both hoping that those Mediterranean waters would not contain any undesirable objects and, with the AA's warning echoing in our ears, we ventured in for our first European dip. As the day was hot, it was a welcome break, although on a colder day I'm not sure the water had quite warmed up enough in early June to warrant being submerged for long. We did also notice that many of the locals were looking at us a little strangely as we emerged from the water. We obviously put that down to the magnificent physical shape we must be in, after cycling constantly for over a month. As we were the only swimmers that day, maybe we'd missed that warning sign which the AA had mentioned, or they could merely have been wondering who the two strangers were, and why were they going for a swim that early in the season.

There was only one way to celebrate our first dip in the Mediterranean and that was with another of those magnificent gelati. The Italians had a flavour called *malaga*, which we knew as rum and raisin, and for the equivalent of sixty-five pence, I had a creation that included a chocolate-rimmed cornet, with *malaga*, lemon, and melon. Jenny again defaulted to a superbly rich chocolate ice cream flavour. Of course, we realised that we had just pre-empted our evening meal with dessert, but when we returned to the camp site, we figured – 'when in Rome …', or at least, Alassio – and we cooked up a large bowl of ravioli for the second day running. The day finished with a conversation with the camp site manager about the potential for reverse charge calls in Italy. We conducted the discussion in French, as a common language, which was something I never expected to be saying. Anyway, it seemed that there was bad news. He didn't think reverse charge calls were possible from Italy, which seemed odd, but we guessed he would know better than us. We'd give it a try at our next large town, but it could be back to aerograms again.

The next day it was apparent that the Italian weather gods were no more convinced than their French celestial cousins that it was early summer, so we decided to stay another day. We in turn hadn't been entirely convinced by the previous conversation about the absence of reverse charge calls in Italy. So, we took a short and very pleasant bike ride into a town called Albenga, which was just along the Ligurian coast. When we arrived and found the post office, I was starting to understand why some unkind people told us before we arrived there that: 'Italy doesn't work very well.' While our frustrations with the PCV service in France were high, they stemmed mostly from the attitude of the customer-service representatives, my inability to understand French when spoken at the speed of light, and my own slower language skills in reply. But at least when we could get through, the service worked. In Italy, it seemed, we couldn't find any way to make reverse charge calls because that system either didn't work or didn't exist. Something I was finding hard to accept because, after all, we were using the same technology, the same phone lines and in 1984, even though we didn't have the internet, this wasn't exactly rocket science. We would have to wait and try again somewhere larger, like Genoa.

On a positive note, having retreated to the camp site for a midday feast, we decided we'd take another long walk into the main town to satisfy the craving for what was fast becoming our new weakness – Italian gelati. Being a Saturday, and moving through the streets on foot, even more slowly than our usual cycling pace, we had the opportunity to observe Italians closely at play – and, among other things, drinking their many variations of coffee. Something that was clearly a serious pursuit.

I was not sure that I would ever be able to fully appreciate life the way Italians did, as I had never acquired the taste for coffee. I realise that puts me in a small minority these days, especially in Australia, where coffee drinking approaches fanaticism in some parts of Sydney and Melbourne. But in 1984 and having grown up in England, it was well known there was no problem or situation, great or small, that a nice cup of tea couldn't solve.

Your home has been bombed by the Luftwaffe. How about a lovely cup of Tetleys?

Your relationship has ended. Fancy a cuppa and a nice Bourbon biscuit?

It's 11 am anywhere in England. Time for a cup of PG Tips and a McVitie's digestive?'

In fact, tea is so important to the British that, during the dark days of World War II, the government allegedly bought all the available black tea in Europe, to be distributed to their troops. They did this as a key mechanism to uphold morale for those soldiers fighting overseas and to remind them of their home. Now *that's* what I call a national passion.

Anyway, on our way into Alassio, we passed many happily feasting families, who were clearly devoting themselves arduously to that very Italian passion of long extended family lunches, with lots of wine. Reflecting on my favourite Italian phrase again, I could see plenty of examples of *mangia bene* and *ridi spesso.* However, I was wondering whether the wine was the reason for the tradition of siestas in Italy, or whether it had something to do with the third component of that saying – *ama molto*. Either way, I certainly had to admit that the Italians had staying power when it came to celebrating and, following a siesta, most of them would be back later that day, dressed in style and out to be seen. They would also be enjoying their *aperitivo,* to 'open their stomachs for dinner'. As an Englishman or Australian, where people at that time tended to mostly eat because they were hungry and needed fuel for the day, the practice of turning almost every meal into entertainment and an occasion was something to which we could aspire. It was early days in our Italian adventure, but the reputation the Italians had as a nation who worked less, spent more time with family, and embraced life and those sharing it with them was certainly well deserved, from what we could tell.

Before we had been distracted by the partying of the locals, we were heading into town to send postcards to my family and as importantly, to obtain what was becoming our daily delicious fix of gelati. This was turning out to be an eventful day though, as we almost didn't make it in one piece. We were quite rudely reminded that, while there were many positives to admire in Italy, there were the occasional traits that could be hazardous to your health, like their driving. I know this could easily be dismissed as another stereotype and I'm sure we in Britain and Australia had our own driving quirks that were confusing for guests in our respective countries. But our experiences in Italy were real, and one of the things we noticed with wry amusement, was that many of the Italian drivers we saw every day were driving quite fast and conducting energetic conversations at the same time. I understood the fast driving in some of the sporty Italian numbers on the road, but that wasn't the main problem. It became potentially hazardous, because the average Italian used both of their hands to gesture for emphasis, as a natural part of speaking, rather than gripping the steering wheel. That did cause us to exercise a degree of caution when we were sharing the roads with them on our bikes, which wasn't necessary in our home countries.

On this occasion though, we were on foot. Which was when we realised that our not unreasonable assumption of safety when using a pedestrian crossing needed to be modified. We experienced many instances of Italian drivers screeching to a halt and waving animatedly at us because we were moving cautiously across the road, not knowing whether they would go past or through us. On this day, a speeding Alfa had literally swerved around us while we were on the pedestrian crossing, and then slowed to enable the driver to lean out of the window and give us what we assumed to be their opinion on our progress. Time for deep breaths and, as we were in Italy, we had to adapt to what felt like a constant game of chicken. I was wondering though, if we were struggling, how did the Swiss and Germans manage when they came to Italy, with their high expectations of rules-based order? Presumably they needed to take the same chill pills as us.

The following morning, we awoke to a familiar overcast day. With no Bureau of Meteorology or handy app to consult in 1984, we decided to throw caution to the wind and rode off towards our next destination. We had only been riding for about 4 kilometres when we realised that we may have misjudged, and the rain started coming down – light at first, but then much more persistent. Surprisingly, though we had seen more than our fair share of rain, this was the first day that we had actually been caught riding in a serious downpour, after more than a month on the Continent. It clearly wasn't the ideal time to stop and socialise with other cyclists, but that was exactly what happened, as we were moving through one town looking for some shelter.

We were passed by a large peloton of racing cyclists. Then 50 metres further on, I heard one call out, '*Scusi*, can I use your pump?' His own was apparently broken, and he borrowed mine gratefully, before motioning me to accompany him. But Jenny had also stopped – to talk with a couple from Vancouver, who were cycling in the opposite direction, on a tandem. This looked interesting and so I motioned back to the Italian racer that he should move off, so he could catch up with his teammates – I think we may have struggled to keep up with him anyway. The Canadian couple looked very fit, and it was also the first time we had seen another female cycle tourist, so we were interested in their journey.

'We've ridden all the way up from Greece and are now going through Italy,' the woman told us. 'But this is the first rain we've seen so far this trip.'

We were hoping that was a good sign for us. They also told us they'd been taking this type of holiday for ten years. No wonder they looked so fit.

As we continued our ride, the weather continued to deteriorate for us, so we stopped at the first town we found to rest and eat, where we inadvertently caused amusement among the passing locals, as we commandeered an outside table of a closed cafe and proceeded to drip all over our picnic lunch, albeit in relative comfort. When we continued our journey, and with visibility rapidly decreasing, as sheets of water poured down on us endlessly, even our waterproof jackets started to struggle. We took every possible opportunity to find shelter along the road, although that was not always easy along the winding, cliffside route. Fortunately, the road tunnels, which were an occasional part of the well-engineered road, were a good place to seek sanctuary from the downpour and give our jackets an opportunity to dry out. It was under one such tunnel, where Jenny was posing glamorously for a photo in her rain gear, that an Italian motorist roared past, tooting his horn and accidentally spraying water all over us. While not really appreciated, it didn't make much difference in the scheme of things, because our clothes, bikes and entire bodies were pretty well soaked through.

On reflection, I might have been the one who suggested, 'It's always sunny in southern Europe so we won't need much rain gear.' Oops!

We'd had enough by mid-afternoon, so we were grateful when we started to see signs for a town called Spotorno, especially because it was one that was recommended by the AA book as having a camp site that was 'pleasantly located … in an orchard at the foot of a hill'. We must have made a sorry sight as we pedalled into a rather deserted camp site. But, having located the office, and deploying my best pidgin Italian, I asked the lady behind the counter whether they had any covered pitches, so we didn't have to assemble our tent in the rain. Apparently not, which was bad news. However, she did ask, in English, 'Would you like a caravan for 10,000 lire a night, for two people?'

'Would we ever … *e grazie mille*!'

That was cheaper than the last camp site. I'm not sure we envisaged that a caravan would be regarded as luxury accommodation when we started the trip, but we were learning that everything was relative. The caravan was not only dry and spacious, but it had a wooden extension attached, in which we could spread our sodden belongings, a table where we could eat a hot meal, and a nice dry bed where we could recover from the day's exertions, without concern over whether our tent would spring a leak. Luxury indeed.

We woke the next day thoroughly refreshed after a hot evening meal and a long, dry and warm sleep – some of Maslow's basic needs satisfied right there. We had particularly enjoyed being in a bed, rather than on a thin rubber sleeping mat, which often ended up barely covering an arrangement of stones. With a break in the weather mid-morning, we decided to stroll into Spotorno and have a look around. It was a lovely, busy town perched on the coast, still in the Golfo di Genova, and we saw plenty of well-stocked pasta shops and pizza parlours, which were teaming with locals. Jenny continued her important research into the gelati of the Italian Riviera and, as she tucked into the inevitable *gelato al cioccolato,* I innocently asked: 'Do you think you may end up with a narrow perspective?'

'What do you mean?' she said.

'Well, you only seem to be ordering chocolate ice cream everywhere we go.'

Although I could tell that she sincerely appreciated my concern, apparently, she was going for depth of understanding rather than breadth. Fair enough.

Strolling around the town, we stopped to watch several expert pasta makers plying their trade inside the shops. It all looked very impressive, and we felt we had to sample some of that locally made spaghetti, matched with their home-made tomato-based sauce later that night. Which left us with the afternoon to amuse ourselves playing games of various kinds, before a very tasty Italian dinner, local wine and off to a dry and comfy bed for the second night in a row. As the Yorkshiremen in the *Monty Python* sketch would say, 'Looxury!'

The next day continued the damp trend, but it was starting to brighten up between showers, so we took another walk into town. We hadn't realised that we would provide quite the level of entertainment for the locals when the day started. But it was quickly becoming apparent that our Italian language skills were not sufficient for all our needs, and Jenny's arms were starting to tire, with all of the gesturing she was being obliged to undertake as a physical translator. It should have been easy as we only needed to buy two packs of playing cards for our amusement and some pasta and pastry for dinner – we had certainly pivoted very quickly from the French to the Italian cuisine.

'How hard can it be to find playing cards?' I said before we set out.

Not very hard to locate a shop that sold them fortunately, although they weren't cheap, at 5,000 lire. So, when we got outside and opened them, we were a little surprised to find that there were only forty cards in the deck, when we expected fifty-two. We hadn't realised that it was quite usual for the Italians, and also the Spanish and Portuguese to use forty-card decks, often referred to as 'stripped decks'. Of course, we only discovered this once we had opened the cellophane and taken out the cards and we definitely needed two decks with fifty-two cards plus jokers for the game we had in mind. So, back into the shop I went to explain the problem, in Italian, and to negotiate for a return of our money. Which, to be fair to them, they happily gave us, even though we had opened the deck.

Then, into another shop where I proceeded to completely confuse the poor shop owner, who must have thought I was crazy, as I kept asking whether there were indeed fifty-two cards in the deck. Because my Italian was clearly quite poor, he thought I was haggling over the price, which was only 1,000 lire. He obviously didn't realise that, as an Englishman I wouldn't have dreamed of doing that anyway – we always assumed the price was the price advertised. Maybe that's why the English were such popular tourists because the locals certainly haggled … a lot.

We then turned our attention to food, and we passed a bread and pastry shop that we had been into the day before, and where I had thoroughly confounded the poor lady behind the counter, by trying to pay for the weight of the bread, which was showing on the till. She couldn't work out why I wanted to pay her six-hundred lire for a loaf of bread and there was much good-natured hilarity from her, and her customers, as I tried to find an English or French translator, and she tried to explain to me in Italian. We got it right this day and brought some cream pastries as well.

The lovely lady behind the counter then called the young man who was evidently both the pastry chef and owner, and who spoke some French. We chatted for fifteen minutes, while he plied us with delicious free samples. I realised then that he thought we were French, and he was very surprised when we told him we were Australian and English. I'd like to think that was because our French was so good, but I fear he may not have been as accomplished in French as he thought. We then found another very helpful lady in a pasta shop where we were intrigued to find large, green sheets of uncut pasta, which had been impregnated with spinach, and were being cut to whatever size and style the customer wanted. This was new for us, but we were helped by the patient explanation of the young assistant, and we bought a sizeable amount for our dinner later that night.

After we had finished confusing and bemusing the local shopkeepers, we bumped into a fellow cycle tourist – a nice young Aussie guy who was also cycling around Europe and staying at the same camp site, 'Rustia'. We were all pleased to find someone who spoke English and he came back to our little hut for a chat, where we discovered that he had cycled across the Alps from Grenoble with another character he had met. That sounded full-on, but we were impressed. After he left, it was time for dinner and Jenny was very keen to try the new 'green' spaghetti, so she gamely cooked a tasty spaghetti carbonara, which she had heard about but neither of us had tried before. I've found that food is often better when you know the 'provenance' – we had watched the artisan make it in the shop only a few hours previously, and it didn't disappoint. Although, as Jenny pointed out: 'The real artisan is the chef!'

I wasn't arguing and, after that it was only fair that I should take on the washing-up. Then, because earlier in the day I had made the tactical error of teaching Jenny to play canasta with our newly acquired fifty-two card decks, she had dealt the cards and was waiting expectantly with a cup of tea, for me to join her.

We liked Spotorno and we also liked being dry and warm, so we were staying for another night, which meant we could play cards until very late before retiring, which was good because canasta can be a *looong* game. Then to cap off a very interesting day, in which we had unintentionally entertained the local shop owners and customers, we were lulled to sleep by the not-so-gentle sounds of a domestic argument at full volume. We weren't sure where it was but given the Italian love of a full-throated and passionate discussion, it could have been anywhere from next door to San Remo.

The following morning, we decided that bike maintenance and food would be the order of the day. On the former, we were surprised to find that there were no bike shops in this town, or at least none that anyone could point us towards. So, the *Readers Digest* bicycle maintenance book would finally earn its place in our panniers, we hoped. The main challenge we were having was that, as we cycled every day, the gears needed adjusting, because they were not changing properly. According to our trusty bicycle maintenance guide, there were several parts of the bike that needed to be adjusted in unison to achieve the outcome we needed – the chain guide, the alignment of the front and rear sprockets, and the carrier mechanism. The problem was also likely to be that we needed to take a few links out of our gear chains, which I didn't have the tools to achieve. I managed to adjust Jenny's so they worked better, but then made a complete pig's ear of my own – so now instead of failing to find fifth and tenth gear, which I could live with downhill, I was unable to find second or first gear. A more worrying problem when we hit the mountains unless I could sort it out or find a bike shop in another town.

At least Jenny's gears were working better, and I figured if I couldn't sort mine, I'd just have to work a bit harder uphill. It looked like I would have to add the Readers Digest to that list of organisations I'd be writing to about their book, when we returned to England. Although they would probably justifiably claim user error. To complete our service, we were able to borrow some oil from the kind Aussie cyclist to give our chains and cables the once over, and to deal with the rust that had started appearing due to the consistently wet weather. It didn't seem fair to impose and delay him before he rode off by asking if he could also help adjust my gears.

On to the food portion of the day as our reward. We found our way back to our favourite pastry shop, which wasn't hard because we just had to follow the queue of locals. Well, a 'queue' would be a generous description of what we encountered at the shop. The pastry chef clearly had a good head for business and his customers' needs, giving away small, free samples to anyone who wanted them, and his shop was always full as a result. But, when I cast my eyes over the locals crowding into the shop, I commented to Jenny, 'I think we should call it a "press" of people rather than a queue.'

Despite my attempts to embrace the laid-back Italian attitudes, I was finding this aspect of Italian life tricky, because anyone who had been brought up in an Anglo-influenced culture implicitly understood the concept of queuing – in person, in a car, or frankly in any situation. They also typically had little patience for anyone 'jumping' a queue, especially when they were standing in it – small wars had been known to break out if someone transgressed. So, when confronted with an entire country for whom queueing was a vague concept that was honoured more in the breach than the observance, I was initially appalled. But needs must and, when we realised that queueing was entirely optional and, what's more, that my six-foot three-inch frame gave us a decided advantage over most of the more diminutive locals, we adapted quite well.

We were able to migrate to the front of the 'press' of people quite easily and none of the locals seemed to take offence. We were also experienced at ordering there now, and our new skills allowed us to clear a handy space to select our ten cakes and collect the obligatory freebies from our friendly chef. Not bad for 1,450 lire, which was the equivalent of fifty-five pence. Loaded up with dessert, we found our favourite pasta shop, where we repeated the 'queueing' technique, and left with armfuls of spaghetti, house-made tomato sauce and *parmigiano.*

'Shopping for food in Italy is fun,' I said to Jenny. 'Once you realise it's a bit like a game of rugby!'

'Yes, but I especially like the part where we get to eat our purchases!' she replied.

Good point, I thought. But we'd need to start cycling seriously again soon, or we would have to add a lot more air to our back tyres, given the rate at which we were consuming the local delicacies. And it was raining again, so we invited our freshly cleaned and serviced bikes into the hut for the night.

The next day still looked uninviting weather-wise, so we persuaded ourselves that we had to spend another night in our warm and cosy hideaway. On a brighter note, though, it gave us the chance to explore Genoa, without worrying about the traffic, or where we could leave our bikes safely.

After a train ride into Genoa for about fifty minutes, we were able to head for the Amex offices to pick up mail, from Jenny's sister and her friend in Paris, and then to the telephone exchange to try to connect live with Oz and the UK. Jenny managed to get through to the family of a friend who would be in London when we returned, so she could let her friend know when we would be arriving. But, when she tried to call her own mum, they told us that there was a cable broken somewhere and calls to Australia were not possible. Really? Apparently, the cables were intact to the UK, and I managed to place a call to fill my dad in on our movements and our progress, and to wish him well for their much-anticipated trip to Canada to visit my mum's twin sister.

Feeling that we had done our family duty and let them know we were still in one piece, we then had time to briefly explore Genoa on foot, before our train took us back to Spotorno. We wandered down to the port through what I would describe as 'character-filled streets, and streets filled with characters'. It was a working port and some of those back streets looked like they doubled as the red-light district. Not the cleanest place we had been, but then most large ports have that flavour to them. It had clearly been there for quite some time – since the Roman Empire, it turns out. But the most amazing thing for me about Genoa was that, during the twelfth and thirteenth centuries, it had been a major maritime and trading power, rivalling Venice and some nation states. They had plenty of 'client' states and cities at that time, even ruling over Constantinople. I'd clearly not been paying enough attention in history lessons, but you could certainly see the remnants of those periods of wealth and prosperity. We only saw a fraction, including the black-and-white striped facade of the grand Cattedrale di San Lorenzo, the Palazzo Ducale and many other impressive buildings opening up onto what must once have been very grand piazzas.

Unfortunately, we needed to cut our wandering short and sprint for the train, only just making the connection to Spotorno. As we arrived back fairly late and were feeling lazy, we headed out to a small but very cosy family restaurant. It's worth pointing out here, as context for our experience, that while Italian restaurants are now everywhere in London and Sydney, this wasn't so much the case in the 1980s. And, even if they were there, it hadn't been either of our families' traditions to eat out at those places. In the UK at least, we satisfied ourselves with an irregular family outing to the local Berni Inn steakhouse for a mixed grill as a special treat, or when older, to the local Indian restaurant for a chicken tikka or rogan josh. So, as a result, we weren't familiar then with most of the classic Italian dishes that we now take for granted, apart from the ubiquitous home-cooked spaghetti bolognaise, obviously. This would explain our 'lost in translation' moment, which almost resulted in a short career as dishwashers, to pay off our bill at the restaurant. Feeling hungry after a day out and about on foot, we chose to start with a large pizza *quattro stagioni* to share – we were on safe ground there, pizzas being plentiful in both Sydney and London. We followed this with a mixed seafood dish, *fritto misto*, and our newly emerging favourite, spaghetti carbonara, washed down with a litre of Frascati.

We'd also spotted a 'salad' display, so in our average Italian we asked, '*Scusi cameriere.* The salad display, is it *gratuita*?' To which the waiter replied, '*Si, naturalmente.*'

Excellent, we thought, we need more veggies in our diet, so we got stuck in. Oops! It turned out that the salad was indeed free, but *not* the thinly sliced seafood and meats that were next to it and which we also mistakenly consumed. We had just discovered antipasti. Something we all take for granted now, but in our less well-travelled gastronomic experience at that time, we had no idea. After we received the bill, we sat there for a few minutes trying to work out whether we had enough cash to pay for it, and we didn't. So, we had to explain to the waiter, who was quite understanding and who reduced the meal to an amount that we could pay. Clearly, we looked trustworthy, and it was good news because that meant we wouldn't need to disappear out the back and wash up a few dozen dishes. The whole meal ended up costing us about 25,000 lire, or nearly eleven pounds sterling, which we thought was pretty good value for the amount we ate and drank.

The next morning, as part of our adjustment to the European way of life, we were enjoying bread and jam for breakfast, which we procured on a 'mercy dash' to the local shop, having eschewed the more traditional Anglo cereal and milk. In most cases it was generally easier than hunting for cereal – the bread was always fresh, reliable, and easily available; and cereal didn't seem to be a popular way to start the day in most of Europe. Refreshed, we were able to get away quickly. We were reluctant to leave our cosy home away from home, but we needed to keep going and the day was clearing, with sun and blue sky even making an appearance – something we hadn't seen for about a week. We struck some steep hills early, but seemed able to manage them more easily than previous days; in fact we were raring to keep going – we must have stored some serious carbs and energy from that meal the night before.

This turned out to be another sociable cycle-tourist day, as almost every time we stopped, we encountered other cyclists along the way. The first of these were a couple of middle-aged, Italian men who came over to chat to us when we stopped to recover at the top of the hill – I think we'd call them mamils today. They wanted to know, in quite good English: 'Where 'ave you come from? Where are you going? 'Ow long will you be cycling in Europe?'

They were both friendly and *very* chatty, but in the end, we elected not to tell them our life stories in response to their questions. Although we did feel a little rude when we eventually rode off with them waving and calling to us as we went, '*Buona fortuna*!'

As Genoa came into view, we paused at a spot overlooking the sea, for a break and a bite to eat, where we met our second cycle tourist of the day – this time an American who was cycling solo, going the opposite way round to the route we were taking. We each took photos, so we could prove we weren't the only crazy people who were undertaking such a trip that summer. We then passed another four pairs of cycle tourists.

'None of these cyclists are women,' Jenny pointed out.

I wasn't arguing and I didn't think this was the time to remind her that this form of transport had actually been her idea. Although she was becoming used to Italian cars slowing down to toot and wave as they weaved past her. We thought there might be a few reasons for that – she was virtually the only female we had seen riding a bike, let alone a touring bike with panniers; she was fit, tanned, and moving slowly, which was an obvious target for Italian male gestures of admiration; and she had sewn the British and Australian flags onto the rear of our panniers the previous night. The latter clearly resonating with many of the Italian locals, who called out 'Aussie!' from time to time, as they passed us, or as we slowly cycled past them.

We made it to Genoa, but it took about two hours to navigate through the streets from one side to the other. During that crossing, we were again treated to driving displays that would earn the individuals concerned a few points off their licence in either the UK or Oz, if there were any police around. Mind you, the police we saw that day were mainly on bicycles. Very Italian, we thought, but they weren't going to be catching those speeding motorists any time soon. It was all very good-natured though, and we were used to it by now, so we weren't feeling threatened. We eventually reached a place called Nervi, on the other side of Genoa and, as the AA book still wasn't covering itself in glory, we popped into a tourist office to ask for the closest place where we might safely pitch our tents.

'Oh, you want to try Bogliasco, it's only 3 kilometres away,' they advised us confidently.

'Outstanding, and e *grazie mille*,' we replied.

We thought we'd understood most of what they were saying,

but if they mentioned the hill on which the camp site was built, we hadn't heard it. The climb was vertical and there was no chance we could ride up it, even if all our worldly goods weren't strapped to our bikes, which of course they were. So, we pushed our bikes uphill for thirty minutes to get to the camp site, where we were relieved to find they had room and a level pitch on the side of a very steep hill, with spectacular views. We worked out we had cycled 85 kilometres in the day, so it was no wonder we were feeling a little weary.

As we settled into our camp site, we met our final fellow tourists for the day – four Canadians who were moving through Europe at pace, in a car. One week previously, they had been in Amsterdam, now they were on the Italian Riviera, whereas we had moved about 150 kilometres in the same time. Listening to their story though, we were feeling pleased that we hadn't tried to stretch our budgets to buy a VW Kombi van, or that could have been our experience, which would have been altogether too rapid. Reflecting on our ride that day, despite it being tiring and involving some considerably bigger mountains than we had anticipated, we'd had a very sociable time – a theme that recurred throughout our trip. Because of the speed of our travel and our easy accessibility to pedestrians or those passing us, we were often hailed to stop for a chat, as we had been that day by Italians, Americans, Canadians, and an English expat. It was making the journey more interesting as a result.

Following the efforts of the previous day's mountainous ride, we had unsurprisingly slept very soundly and, by the next morning, we'd recovered quickly from our ride. That was probably due to a combination of that deep sleep, our relative youth, and the increasing fitness and endurance we were building each day.

Feeling pleased with ourselves, but a little sweaty having just crashed the night before, I trotted up the hill to a lone shower cubicle with my coins for a hot shower and, unknowingly, it was my turn for a random shower experience. Although this would be without the uninvited amphibian that Jenny had experienced in France. I'd just covered myself from head to toe with soap, when the water stopped … completely. No hot *and* no cold. This was a new experience and there was only one thing for it.

I stuck my head outside the door and called, 'Jennyyyy!'

I thought I had used a reasonably subdued tone, to try to catch her attention in our tent, 30 metres down the hill. Not quite as subdued as I had intended, apparently, to the amusement of several other campers, who poked their heads out of their tents to see what the fuss was about. Fortunately, Jenny was the only one who actually came up to investigate. Several minutes later, and trying, though failing, to suppress a fit of the giggles, she came back with a bowl of cold water and a hand towel so I could de-soap and finish my 'shower'. We were used to the hot water stopping and needing to finish off with a cold shower, but stopping all the water seemed a bit extreme. I guess I deserved the reaction from Jenny, given the limited sympathy I had shown her when our positions had been reversed in France.

We definitely needed some energy enhancers after our ride of the previous day, so we walked down from our perch in the clouds, descending several hundred steps to the town, where we found a shop selling Italian meringues in bags. Excellent, we thought, and I deployed my best Italian accent to order.

'*Cento grammo, per favore.*'

We didn't really need 100 grammes of meringues, which ended up being ten each, but boy did they taste good, and they gave us the same sugar hit we'd experienced from our bars of chocolate in France. Jenny then popped into a grocer while I guarded the meringues outside, but she walked out of the shop with a lot more food than we could possibly consume.

'I think you've got someone else's shopping,' I said.

'Don't be silly,' she replied.

But then she realised that she did indeed have two bags of food, one of which belonged to a fellow shopper, who had been chatting to the shop owner when Jenny checked out. She rushed back in, to general laughter all round. Jenny could get away with that, but I'm not sure I would have received the same reaction.

We staggered back up the hill to our camp site, grateful we weren't also carrying someone else's heavy shopping, where Jenny decided that the Italian custom of a siesta warranted exploration and went for a lie-down in the tent. I pottered around outside with the bikes, and as I was sitting there looking at the view, I said to myself, 'If this cloud comes much lower, we will be sitting in it.'

Fortunately it didn't, and as we sat there in the early evening, reflecting on the last few days, we had a truly spectacular vista over the pastel-coloured town of Bogliasco and the impressively clear waters of the Ligurian sea.

'Our life's not shit, is it?' I said.

'*Assolutamente*!' Jenny replied, gesturing like an Aussie Rules umpire, for emphasis.

We awoke, relieved that we *weren't* sitting in the clouds the next morning. We packed up quickly and headed off to our next destination, Sestri Levante. It was a Sunday, and the roads were swarming with people – in cars, on motor bikes and on scooters. We knew the next leg would engage the lower gears on our bikes, as we were skirting the base of very tall mountains and eventually the Italian engineers would run out of space and would need to head upwards. This happened at a town called Recco, where the road climbed quickly and steeply, to the top of the mountain at Ruta. Even though we were quite fit by now, we still walked a fair portion of the 4 kilometres upwards, pushing our bikes in front. When we eventually made it to the top, the views were rewarding and genuinely spectacular. We thought we could see right down to the headland, which contained a beautiful town called Portofino, nestled into the point. A popular and well-known tourist destination these days, but then it would have involved an even more mountainous route – so we wouldn't be going there on this trip.

As we were taking in the beauty of the surroundings, an older Italian cyclist, who was built like a Turkish wrestler and had calf muscles the size of tennis balls, stopped to chat, in a combination of French, Italian and English. He was very friendly, unlike many of the reflecto-wearing youngsters we had passed during our ride that day, who gave us a series of blank stares when we waved. Oh well, their loss. Anyway, he was empathising about the hill we had both just climbed, especially when he looked at all the gear we had on our bikes, and he warned us, 'There is another big 'ill coming soon!'

And he was right, though this one was only 3 kilometres to the top and then down again, very fast, all the way to Chiavari. It's amazing the speed you can achieve on a bike when you are loaded up with gear and you don't touch the brakes much. We even overtook a couple of slow-cruising scooters on the way down, much to their surprise and then amusement as we swerved past them, calling out '*Attento*!', to make sure they knew we were there.

We had stopped earlier to eat some lunch at a shop we had noticed, and which was unexpectedly open, on the way down from Ruta, on the first hill – open, on a Sunday, in a Catholic country! We were pleased they were, and we were able to eat in the brilliant sunshine, while overlooking a small town nestled in a bay in the distance.

'This isn't a bad way to spend a Sunday,' I said, as we relaxed from our climb.

When we reached the flat, we didn't need to stop to refuel our bodies and could keep going until we reached Sestri Levante. Again, our camping advisors didn't have any suggestions to offer here in their directory, so we had to check out the camp sites ourselves. The first looked a little run-down from the outside, so we went to see what else was available, riding another 8 kilometres in the process. Before eventually deciding that the first camp site was the one most in our price range. It turned out to be a good decision once we rode into the grounds, because it had only just been opened for the summer, was freshly painted and cleaned and, for 8,900 lire a night, was more in our price range. There was also a very convenient shop on the premises. So, tired after our long and hilly ride, we bought and cooked our usual staple of pasta, found a hot shower and crashed for what we hoped would be a long sleep.

Of course, hope is not a strategy and I slept quite badly. But I was woken in the morning from a light sleep by Jenny singing in my ear.

'Happy birthday to you,
Happy birthday to you,
Happy birthday, dear Stevie …'

You get the drift. As I tried to shake myself awake, Jenny trotted off to the shops and reappeared with a veritable breakfast feast – milk chocolate, fresh milk, and half-a-dozen fresh pastries. After we had gorged ourselves and replenished our energy stocks, we cycled into town to scout out the territory for restaurants for the evening. Finding a couple of likely candidates, we then rode around the seafront while demolishing *malaga* and chocolate ice creams, and stocked up on some beers and nibbles to see us through to dinner. It was going to be a tough day!

When we emerged from the tent later that afternoon, after a few beers and an afternoon lie-down, I finally understood why Jenny had packed the red high-heeled shoes. I appreciated the effort and, as it turned out, so did the local men. She attracted a fair share of male attention as we walked along the waterfront to the restaurant, one of whom apparently pinched her bottom lightly as he passed – an action that was not acceptable as far as we were concerned, either then or now. But the older Italian men were known for such acts, and it was apparently seen as a sign of appreciation. That said, Jenny chose not to tell me until later, which was wise, because I may not have been so forgiving if I had known.

Anyway, despite this unwanted attention, we arrived at our selected restaurant, which was a very cosy little family-run place. As we walked in, we were instantly wrapped in an inviting blanket of hospitality and we were greeted by our host, who looked like he had stepped straight from central casting on *The Godfather* movie franchise.

'*Buonasera e benvenuti signore e signora*,' he said warmly. 'Please sit 'ere while I get your menus,' he continued, as he showed us to a corner table.

Already loosened up by our pre-dinner beers and disarmed by the hospitality and the easy way the host switched from Italian to English, we proceeded to order and eat a very large meal – shared pizza *quattro stagioni* to start, followed by house-made spaghetti, then Italian ice cream, washed down with a litre of their house Frascati. All for the reasonable cost of 34,000 lire, which was about fifteen pounds sterling. It was more than our normal daily allowance – but it was a special occasion with good Italian cooking, it had a very comforting feeling about it, and we didn't do it often.

A middle-aged Norwegian lady at a nearby table started talking to us, and said that she was with her husband, who was there on business. After about fifteen minutes' conversation, she started loudly regaling her whole table with the story of the young couple next to her, who were touring Europe on bikes for two years. Jenny had been explaining to her that she was over in the UK and Europe from Oz for two years and it became lost in translation. It was too hard to explain, so we took the plaudits and admiring glances, paid our bill gratefully and walked slowly back to our tent.

When we arrived, just before midnight, we were being tracked by hundreds of small insects that were seemingly putting on a display for us, flashing lights on and off like multiple Christmas trees. Although, in retrospect, we had consumed quite a lot of beer and wine, so maybe there were half the number of insects we thought. Either way, it was an entertaining end to a delightful day and a unique way to spend my birthday. I was feeling very spoilt.

The following day, we were feeling rather fragile after the alcoholic efforts of the night before – something we weren't really used to on this trip. The weather was fine again though, and we made use of it to undertake essential tasks, such as our washing. After all, cycling can be a very sweaty business. Having completed this exercise with almost our entire travelling wardrobe, I was now confident that the locals could comfortably sit or stand downwind from me in restaurants and shops, and we could head into town. Jenny of course only 'perspired lightly', or 'glowed', apparently, so it hadn't been a problem for her. We found a friendly bike-shop owner who was more than happy to chat with a couple of cycle tourists from over the water and, while he was doing so, with a couple of turns of a screwdriver in the appropriate places, he had adjusted my gears so I could use them all. A great improvement and apparently at no charge – very kind of him, as he could easily have made it more difficult and charged me an arm and a leg for the privilege. Clearly there is honour among cyclists.

It was turning out to be another social day, as was often the case when we slowed down or stopped in towns and took the time to engage with people – one of the ongoing benefits of cycling through Europe, despite my whingeing about the mountains. We did find ourselves regularly talking to locals on the trip, and Jenny told me that was because I was a 'social butterfly'. Guilty as charged, but my view was that, if we were open and talked to people when they were prepared to engage, we not only improved our knowledge of the places we were seeing and the people we were meeting, but our language skills improved too. Talking with people wherever we might be had always been one of the more interesting aspects of travel, as far as I was concerned, even more so when in a different language.

In that vein, we were stopped by a retired English couple who apparently visited this port in June and September of every year, because they moored their boat there – that was a retirement goal to file away for future reference. Returning to the camp site, we then started chatting to a couple who were a similar age to us – a German called Peter and his Italian girlfriend, Josey. She had an Aussie passport, having lived there for seven years, but was based with him in Germany. And we thought we were a multicultural couple – we were clearly amateurs. Anyway, they were travelling around Europe in a car, had seen the Aussie flag on Jenny's pannier and had an offer for us.

'We're driving to the Cinque Terre today,' Josey said. 'And we wondered if you'd like to come along with us?'

We were peripherally aware of those five famous towns, because they are on a mountainous outcrop of land around the coastline, which due to the scale of our route planner, had not been labelled individually but rather as a group, shown as '*Cinqueterre*'. We had thought we wouldn't be able to get there and back easily on our bikes and camping wasn't really an option, so we had dismissed the idea on this trip. But, with transport and some friendly fellow tourists offering to take us there and back, we thought it was our lucky day – those flags on our panniers continued to pay for themselves. Not much of a decision to make there, so Jenny replied for both of us.

'Thanks very much for the offer. We would love to join you.'

Once we had loaded the car with beers and wine for the trip, along with a few nibbles, we all piled into their Volkswagen and off we went. The drive there was a continuation of a theme for this part of Italy – amazing civil engineering winding around the side of mountains, with sheer drops to the right, when we weren't speeding through the long tunnels that had been carved out of the rock. When we finally started descending, it was on a switchback-like road, which wound its way down from the mountains into the larger of the five towns, Monterosso, which sat nestled in the bay against a long, sandy beach. We later discovered that vehicle access, if not prohibited, was strongly discouraged to the other four towns of the Cinque Terre, with paths and trains running between the five connected locations.

We managed to find a place to park the car on the outskirts of this town and, after we had strolled down to the front, we discovered a collection of restaurants that opened almost directly onto the road, and were situated opposite the main beach. It was early evening by the time we had driven the 50 kilometres from Sestri Levante and so, being hungry, we walked into the first restaurant we saw – largely because of the man who was expansively engaging passers-by and hawking for trade in front of his establishment. He'd spotted that we were not Italian, except Josey, of course, and engaged us in fluent English; asking us where we lived, regaling us with tales of his house in Kent, and telling us that he had the best wine in the Cinque Terre. Quite a claim, given the region was famous for producing its own very good wines. Once we were inside and committed, he cheekily told us that he drinks the best himself, but that even the ones left over were better than anything else we had drunk before.

'What, even better than Blue Nun or Black Tower Liebfraumilch?' I asked him, with my tongue firmly planted in my cheek.

I'd forgotten that in Italy, like in America, English irony did not always translate. So, we had to listen to a five-minute rant about those inferior wines and the general superiority of Italian wines, full stop.

'Okay,' said Peter. 'Prove it to us!'

'Well played, Peter,' I said quietly, and added to our host, 'If it's good enough, we'll have two bottles please, but we don't want to spend too much.'

I didn't think that would be a problem, as the restaurant and wine list weren't going to feature in the Michelin guide any time soon. Though it was very clean, and the owner clearly cared about his customers, despite his bravado. So off he strode to find a couple of bottles of his best Cinque Terre wine that would rise to the challenge from this multinational table – and our table did resemble the opening line to a joke: 'So, a German, an Englishman, an Australian and an Italian walk into a bar …'

Josey, who probably knew a thing or two about Italian wines, confided: 'This will be interesting now that we've called his bluff – we'll either get a great bottle of wine, or he won't be coming over to our table again tonight!'

And our host clearly hadn't been joking about his wines, because he did in fact find two very drinkable bottles of local white for us, white being the region's specialty, and at a reasonable price. The first of which we gladly polished off with our tasty spaghetti dishes and the second, an excellent dessert wine called *Sciacchetra* we consumed with the restaurant's house-made nut cake. Then, because it was such a lovely town, we decided we'd hang around and watch the moon rise. So, we retrieved a couple of bottles of red wine from Peter's car, along with some local cheese, bread and meat, found some empty deckchairs on the sandy beach, and set up to watch the moon put on a display, while we continued our gastronomic journey. It was a full moon and as the light was bouncing off the waters, Jenny sat back and pronounced contentedly, 'This is the life … we could be in an Italian tourism advertisement.'

So classically beautiful was the setting. We sat there chatting, finishing off our second feast in four hours, watching the prawn boats bobbing up and down on the horizon and enjoying the show. Sure, we may have been affected by the fact we had each drunk at least a bottle of wine, but some moments seem almost perfect, and this was one of them, so we were sitting back and revelling in it – until it started to get cold.

I don't completely recall the trip back to our camp site, but now I think about it, that may be a good thing. After all, Peter had just drunk a lot of wine and beer and we were travelling along those very same windy roads, with vertical drops now just off to our left. Did I mention it was 1984? Not terribly responsible, but then not unusual. We finally made it into our joint camp site by 2am, when Jen and I filed off into our own tent and crashed. This was the second night in a row we had been drinking until late and it was starting to feel a little like a rugby tour, though without the punishing sport in between drinking sessions, and with much more pleasant company.

We were up late again and very much the worse for wear the next day. Fortunately, we had bread and jam left over from the previous day's brekkie and so no 'mercy dash' was needed to the local shops. Our bodies needed time to recover, though, before we hit the road and mountains, so we spent the day lying around and sleeping in the sun, with a couple of sorties, for dinner and to send postcards for Father's Day. This time we tried a new pasta – to us at least. Tortellini in a cream and tomato paste sauce. We were broadening our culinary experiences, but my notes at the time suggest that my taste buds had some way to go before making it worth our while to venture into any Michelin-starred restaurants.

After I'd taken a few bites of the tortellini, I said to Jenny, 'This tastes a bit like pork pies, but less spicy!'

Clearly, I needed to widen my culinary comparators, which after all, was part of the point of this trip. I probably needed to work on my tact as well, given she had just spent half an hour preparing it for us on one gas ring! Oh well, time to rest those weary muscles in the hope of an early start to tackle the large mountains the next day.

When the alarm went off at 6:30 am, we looked at each other, poked our heads outside the tent and decided we needed more rest. So, we climbed back into our sleeping bags and grabbed a few more hours of badly needed 'zeds'. The weather seemed to have turned for the better and it was heating up nicely, so we jumped onto our trusty bikes and headed for a ride along the seafront, to find a suitable beach where we could relax for the day. The area's nickname is the 'Bay of Silence', and it's known for providing inspiration over the years for luminaries as varied as Hans Christian Andersen and the scientist Guglielmo Marconi. The general feel of the place was pretty chilled and a little eclectic – with scores of multicoloured beachfront houses, built with no thought about rising seas and literally opening from the front doors onto the main beach. Picturesque though it all was, Jenny's verdict after we had cycled the entire length and passed multiple small beaches was: 'I'm not sure I want to lie on any of those!'

And who was I to argue. After all, when it comes to being a

connoisseur in the beach department, it was hard to overrule a Sydneysider, who had easy access to some of the world's most beautiful beaches. She did also have a point, as they were either seaweed-infested, or dotted with yesterday's tourist-rubbish. So, we chose some very large and flat rocks behind one of the beaches, laid out our towels and stayed there for around four hours catching more 'bennys'. At one point, Jenny made a run for ice creams back to the camp site and in the process the guy running the shop seemed to be giving her a hard time, because we had been buying our groceries at another place down the road. This was purely price-driven, but as he had been quite rude to Jenny, I made sure that when we cooked and ate our goodies from the shop down the road that night, we did so as he was taking his evening stroll around the camp site. Being English, I didn't want to make a scene, but we convinced ourselves that we had taught him a lesson and maybe he would think about his prices.

Later that evening we decided to explore some nearby ancient Roman ruins and took a walk up an old Roman road. It climbed vertically out of the camp site and crossed a steep cliff, to a ruined church: *Rocche di S. Anna* after which the camp site itself had been named. We had seen other archaeological remains in France and Italy on our trip, but this was much more rustic. As we tramped up the slightly overgrown path and trod in the footsteps of the Roman legions who would have marched over those cliffs, on their way to or from various campaigns, we thought we could picture some of the hardships those troops would have encountered – although to be fair, our major hardship was likely to be getting a bit sore, wet, or hungry, not having to face battle the next day. Still, the imagination is a powerful force, aided I am sure by multiple Hollywood movies. When we'd finished our tour of those ruins, we were heading back to camp and I was again hailed by a German, who chatted to me for a while before realising that I had no idea what he was talking about. This would clearly be interesting when we eventually got to Germany, if even the locals assumed that I came from their country.

From reviewing our large map book, we knew that roughly one fifth of Italy was covered in hills and mountains, and the following day we would tackle one of the more notorious along that stretch – Passo del Bracco. So, this time when the alarm went off at 6:30 am, we got up and packed as quickly as we could, so we'd be cycling before the heat of the day. We had been told by several other cyclists that it was very challenging, and even the AA had helpfully warned us that it was, 'A two-lane road with continuous bends, passing usually difficult.'

Excellent, and both the AA and the other cyclists were right – it was 10 kilometres straight up, with multiple winding turns and narrow lanes that offered plenty of opportunity for motorists to gather speed on their way down. It took us three hours to climb it, and I'd like to say that we rode all the way, but in reality, we negotiated a fair bit of the climb on foot, pushing our bikes. I wasn't helped by having foolishly attempted some 'fine-tuning' of my gears the day before, effectively shutting down my options to use first or second gear – again! We did eventually arrive at what we assumed to be the top, where we stopped to eat lunch and admire the expansive views all the way down to the Ligurian Sea. When we pushed on, we realised we hadn't quite reached the summit, because we turned a corner to see the sign displaying, 'Passo del Bracco; m. 615'. It was definitely time to pull out the camera and capture the evidence that we had made it to the top with both of our bikes.

Descending on the other side was a lot more fun and very fast – we made roughly the same distance in thirty minutes and kept pace with a couple of Fiats, with some very handy 'drafting' to ease the wind resistance. I'm not sure we would have tried drafting with, say, a Morris Minor in the UK on a mountain descent, but we had yet to see an Italian driver slow down on the roads, so we figured we could get relatively close and coast behind them. The mountain range was not yet done with us, though, and we had to climb a few smaller mountains where again, the height was not the issue, but the gradients were brutal. Clearly the engineers who built those roads wanted to get to the top in the fastest manner possible, but it was continuing to prove challenging with our loads to cycle all the way up.

After close to 80 kilometres of hard climbing on mostly deserted roads, we reached the major town in the area, La Spezia. We weren't really in the mood to negotiate too much large-town traffic, so as we saw no camping signs, we headed for Lerici where we finally had a camp site from the AA book. On arriving in Lerici we found a tourist bureau that, remarkably, was still open in the early evening, and they informed us that we needed to negotiate another large mountain to reach the camping grounds. After our day, we had no interest in climbing any more hills, so we backtracked to a small town called San Terenzo and found a very comfortable *pensione*, where we parted with the princely sum of 20,500 lire, or about eight pounds sterling. We needed the rest, and it was too late to find a camp site, being nearly 7 pm by the time we arrived there.

We had a short and interesting conversation with the landlady, a formidable-looking Italian *nonna,* about where we could store our bikes safely. It was one thing to lose a water bottle, as we had done on the French Riviera, but quite another to lose our mode of transport. Strangely, she wasn't too keen for us to bring our bikes up into our room, so we negotiated a place in their internal courtyard. With the bikes stored and padlocked, we dumped our gear in our room, looked gratefully at the comfortable bed and traipsed downstairs to top up our energy supplies in their restaurant. They had home-made spaghetti pesto, which was another new variation for us, and we loved it – subtle but very tasty, especially when washed down with a litre of the house red. A wonderful way to end an expected hard day's cycling, and a comfortable bed as a bonus.

We were starting to close in on the part of Italy where we wanted to spend more time, namely Firenze, Roma and Venezia, so we weren't going to stay for long in those smaller towns. Especially because we were also starting to have some concerns in relation to our budget. While we had been living frugally, it was being dented by the occasional 'treats' and the higher-than-hoped-for expenses on the Riviera. We were enjoying those treats and luxuries though.

The next day we were able to exit our *pensione* quickly because there was no need to pack up the tent, which had meant a much-appreciated sleep-in was our reward. We stopped in Lerici again for some water and a map and then, another surprise as we turned the first corner out of town – the longest and straightest hill we had seen so far disappeared into the clouds. We were veterans at this now, though. We just had to put our heads down and keep pedalling, with plenty of encouragement from passing motorists and the occasional racing cyclist who passed us on the way up. We assumed we would keep on climbing, as we had the day before, but we were surprised and delighted to find ourselves cruising downhill for about 4 kilometres at one point. It was so easy that we were able to stop for a quick food break, where we were kept talking by the couple who owned the place, and who were keen for us to reprise our travelling-language-coach roles with their son.

However, we failed to engage their shy young son, and we pushed on to Viareggio on the coast. What a joy it was to be on the flat again, and very fast. We were aiming for a camp site at Torre del Lago, described by the AA as a 'site in pine and poplar woodland' – and cheap by Italian Riviera standards. It was right on the edge of Lago di Massaciuccoli, which is the largest lake in the Tuscan region. We'd covered 60 kilometres in just under four hours and that included a lunch stop for an hour, which was very different to the day before. We were now only 15 kilometres from Pisa, and from there, it would be a longish ride along what appeared to be a river valley, to Florence. The camping ground also had a shop on site, which meant we could spend a day chilling, without having to venture out for supplies, and we could revisit our plan for the next stage of the trip.

Having lived in Australia, we were prepared for heat, but Sydney didn't often have the same humidity we were experiencing in this part of Italy, and especially very close to this large lake. It was rather like being in Northern Queensland, where you'd get up, shower, dress, have breakfast and then feel the need to shower again as the humidity wrapped around you. We've since experienced that in even more concentrated form, when we lived and worked in Hong Kong for several years, however that's a story for another day. But in 1984, it was a new and uncomfortable experience for both of us, especially as much of our day was spent in the saddle of a bike. As we were feeling lethargic and had nominated a 'planning day', we scooted out of our tent to find some fresh rolls for breakfast from the campsite shop, and Jenny persuaded me to try Nutella. By now you may have worked out that chocolate-based treats were a bit of a weakness. I discovered that Nutella tastes okay on bread, but tastes a whole lot better by itself, so the jar didn't last very long. We then spent some time on essential maintenance of our bikes, as the brakes had taken a hammering on the downhills recently, a few cables needed tightening and I had to get first and second gear capability back – a task I finally managed to complete with the support of Readers Digest and their diagrams.

So, to planning. For a start we weren't contemplating cycling over the Alps. Whatever thoughts, or 'fantasy' as Jenny preferred to call it, we might have harboured about the possibility of attempting that bigger range, the idea had been laid to rest during our climb over Passo del Bracco and the various detours through the Maritime Alps and the Apennines. Therefore, we knew we would take the train over the Alps, but we thought stopping for a few days in Switzerland would be worth considering. We wouldn't plan to spend a long time there, but we were both interested to find out if the place was as 'calm' and well-ordered as it had always appeared from the outside.

We also had a close look at the Florence-to-Rome leg and realised we would spend a large amount of both time and money getting down and back from Rome, when really, we would be better spending that time in Florence and Rome themselves. So, we'd hitch or catch a train from Florence to Rome; train back to Venice; over the Alps through Switzerland; to Freiburg, and then, cycling what we hoped would be the more attractive part of the Rhine Valley, to Heidelberg – avoiding the more industrial north and the larger towns. Sounded like a new plan!

Having sorted our route changes, it was time to finish the day and ready ourselves for the next leg. A relaxing shower would be just the ticket. However, one thing we had noticed in Italy was that prices varied, sometimes in one day at the same place, presumably depending on the mood of the proprietor and how their business was doing. For instance, the advertised morning price for a warm shower of 400 lire, had magically doubled in price during the day to 800 lire.

'Oh well,' I said to Jen. 'It's humid and a cold shower will have to do for me tonight!'

We ended the day with another new spaghetti dish, prepared by Jenny – *spaghetti al fungi*. We thought we were becoming quite the connoisseurs of spaghetti dishes, especially ones that could be prepared in our more constrained 'kitchen' facilities, aka a one-gas ring. I also taught Jenny a new card game called euchre, at which she proceeded to beat me, so that would be the last new game I'd be teaching her … back to the Scrabble championships. Not that I'm competitive.

The day finished on something that Jenny now calls my 'dance of the mosquitos' – which gave endless entertainment to her on that trip and has continued to do so over the years. I have always had an aversion to mosquitos, maybe because I seem to attract them more than most people. Jenny says that is due to my delicate English complexion. Whatever the reason, there was nothing worse than the high-pitched buzz of a mosquito in the ear as I was nodding off to sleep and which, when I turned on the light to find it, immediately became invisible. We were by a lake so it was likely we would encounter those little terrors; but now they were in our tent, and I couldn't get to sleep until I had caught them all, which took some time and gymnastic ability on my part. It was 'better than television' apparently!

CHAPTER 7

Pisa and Firenze

The weather pattern had definitely changed. We woke to a gloriously sunny day and I had a new proposition for Jenny.

'Let's cycle to and from Pisa on a day trip. It's only 15 kilometres each way and we can leave our bikes somewhere without all the gear, while we explore the sights.'

She thought that was a good idea but was a little worried about the longer trip to Florence, or to use its Italian name Firenze, the next day. I understood the concern, so I pointed out, 'It's 95 kilometres, but it is mostly flat. It should be fine if we leave early.'

We eventually agreed this was a logical course of action and off we went. It was certainly much more relaxing cycling with only a small backpack, and it was very flat, so we made good time.

Like most of the people who visit Pisa, we were there to explore the Leaning Tower, and it made quite a sight when you first arrived in the precinct. We were busy looking for somewhere to safely lock up our bikes when we were hailed by the same elderly English couple who we had met in Tournon and then

Menton, in France. I guess we stood out with our bikes, but I wasn't sure which they were more surprised at – to see us again, or that we had actually made it that far on our cycling tour. Either way, the lady insisted on taking our photos with our bikes for their holiday album. I'm imagining that somewhere, someone is looking at an album of their parents' trips and asking, 'Who are those fit-looking young people on the bikes?' And of course, no-one will know.

My own parents had one of those mysterious photos, though in a much more important album – from their wedding day. They hadn't noticed until they received the wedding photo book and were poring over the photos, as you did in those days when you received the hard copies. My dad apparently was looking at the groom's family-and-friends photo when he asked, 'Who's the old man at the far end of the back row in the bicycle clips?'

No-one knew. They assumed he must have seen the wedding group as he was cycling past, jumped off his bike and strolled onto the end of the back row, where he had stood with a slightly bemused smile on his face. No-one had noticed and he hadn't bothered or had the time to take off his bicycle clips (which some younger readers won't know were metal in those days and were 'clipped' around your trousers, to stop them flapping in the chain and getting greasy). Fortunately, both my mum and dad had a wonderful sense of humour and thought it was hilarious, as well as being a good story to tell friends … and children when we came along.

But back to Pisa. Jenny decided she had to pose for the classic Pisa photo of her standing on the grass and leaning at a similar angle to the tower in the near distance. And it really did lean – the guidebook told us it was 4.7 metres further out at the top of the tower, than at the bottom. That was one hell of a lean for something that size and weight. The tower has changed somewhat now, but at that time, 'health and safety' in Italy was clearly more of a concept than a reality. As a result, when you reached the tower and walked up the internal stone staircase, you could emerge from a small doorway onto any of the first five levels, which were nothing more than a stone platform, with up to twenty supporting columns rising from the level below. Amazingly, the platforms on those levels had no railings or barrier of any kind that would prevent you from falling. If the tower had been straight, that would have been a little dangerous. But on a tower that leaned over at such an angle, when you turned out of the door to the left, you immediately had to tense back against the circular tower wall, to prevent walking down too fast and straight off the edge. I'm not sure what the statistics were, but I'd have been very surprised if there hadn't been a few unfortunate accidents on that tower before they installed barriers, or stopped tourists walking out onto those levels in later years. I understood that in 1174, when it was built, life was less controlled.

But, as I pointed out to Jenny, 'It's 1984 and they *have had* 800 years to think about the problem, after all.'

At least, by the sixth floor, they had decided to install some railings, but even then, there were still gaps. The seventh floor was completely enclosed, with a low stone wall that seemed to be part of the original design, with railings added. There was then an iron ladder fixed to the wall, climbing vertically to a smaller balcony and belfry, which contained four very large brass bells. They would have made one heck of a noise when rung together. We parted with 3,000 lire for that tour, and we felt it was well worth the money, even though, elsewhere on the grounds, the cathedral with its heavily carved doors, and the baptistry were closed. As we were unlocking our bikes to leave, we started chatting to some other cycle tourists – all men again – a Kiwi and a couple of Americans who had come from Athens, via (what was then) Yugoslavia and Rome and were heading on to London. They were riding to Florence the next day, so we hoped we'd catch up with the Kiwi again, as Jenny was always eager to exchange stories with fellow antipodeans. When we returned to our camp site, we were feeling pretty good, though hot, so we had an invigorating, and free, cold shower, some tuna and rice for dinner and then hit the hay for our long journey the next day.

With nearly 100 kilometres to ride, we were up early so we would have as much time as possible before the real heat of the day, because we knew it was going to be a hot one and there wouldn't be much shade. We wouldn't just have the heat to contend with either: that southern Italian humidity would drain us if we weren't careful.

Once we started, the terrain was flat as we had hoped, but to offset that, the road looked like it hadn't seen any form of maintenance since just after the Second World War. Perhaps they hadn't got around to filling in the holes made by the tanks as they came through – it was shocking and there were potholes everywhere. Tough to avoid some of them on a bike without swerving into the path of speeding motorists, which we were naturally keen to avoid. Despite this, we made reasonable progress, stopping regularly to rehydrate with fruit and drinks and, after 50 kilometres, we felt we had made good enough time to pause for lunch.

Unfortunately, after we started again, the road and potholes took their toll and Jenny's back wheel developed another puncture. We'd experienced a similar problem before and it seemed to be a slow leak, so we figured we could pump it up and limp into our next camp without having to change the tyre. However, every 10 kilometres it would go down again, and we would need to stop, so I could pump it vigorously to allow us to continue. I unloaded some of Jenny's gear onto my bike to lighten the weight on the tyres, but I expected that each time I pumped in more air, I was enlarging whatever small hole was developing on the inner tube. However, this wasn't a great road on which to be changing a tyre, with no real hard shoulder available to shelter from the traffic, so we had to keep moving.

As we reached the outskirts of Florence, a middle-aged Italian, who introduced himself as Stephan, slowed down alongside me on his bike to chat for a while. He told me he was going to the same camp site where we were headed, to meet someone and then get a haircut, and he suggested that we follow him. This was helpful as we weren't completely sure of the way at that point. Jenny's bike wasn't in good shape though, and we had to stop on five more occasions to re-pump the offending tyre. Stephan kindly waited each time, even though we suggested he should continue on his own. What a lovely fellow, we thought. We finally reached the steep hill that would take us up to our camp site at the Piazzale Michelangelo. At that point, Stephan very gallantly gave Jen his lightweight racer and jumped onto her gear-laden bike, to ride it up the hill. He had earlier told me that it was 31 degrees Celsius, and the humidity must have been in the nineties. The poor guy was sweating profusely by the time we reached the top, as were we, but then we weren't dressed in a pair of black trousers and a nice, crisp white shirt. Mind you, by the end, neither was he.

'Thank you *sooo* much!' Jenny said, as she reclaimed her injured bike.

'No problem,' Stephan replied, calling '*Buona giornata*!' as he went off to find his friend.

'What an absolute gentleman!' I said to Jenny.

It's acts of random kindness like that which can make such a difference to your day, and we still remember it fondly more than thirty years later. At the time, we were certainly extremely grateful.

When we two very tired cycle tourists finally rolled into the entrance to the camp site, our first reaction was summed up by Jenny: 'Wow, that view is absolutely amazing!'

The camping ground had a terrific location just below the Piazzale Michelangelo. That was the terrace that commanded one of the most stunning and complete views of Florence, which in turn was laid out in the river basin below, like a medieval toy town. Our second reaction was a little more worrying.

'This camp site looks very full,' I said, 'and I can't see any spare plots.'

It was indeed full, and we had to negotiate quite hard for the owner to allow us to stay. In the end I just told him, in quite strident tones, 'Look, we've just ridden from Pisa, we're tired and we're not leaving tonight.'

I think he took pity on us when he realised how far we had ridden that day, and it was going to get dark quite soon. We also must have looked ragged after riding 95 kilometres in the heat. So, he relented, and told us that we could plant our tent at the very back of the site, which turned out to be on a small slope.

At that point, we couldn't afford to be fussy, so we erected the tent as well as we could, went to grab another cold, but very welcome shower, made a large portion of spag bol and then retired into our tent for a long sleep. After a few minutes we decided that I needed to sleep on the bottom of the slope, so I could act as a barrier for Jenny and so that, if I rolled over, I wouldn't gain momentum and squash her. It was quite a slope, but at that stage, we didn't care and just wanted to sleep, which we did almost immediately.

Florence was one of the places Jenny had been most looking forward to seeing again, having visited it briefly with a friend on an earlier whistle-stop tour, on her way back from the Greek Islands. She had studied art and had an ongoing interest in it, which would be easy to satisfy in Florence, given it has been described by many as an 'open-air museum' – with its many beautiful *piazzas* and palaces. Those spaces were also populated with statues by great Renaissance artists such as Michelangelo, Giambologna, and others. I had less idea of what to expect, so I was receiving a crash course and was pleased to discover that I not only liked but appreciated the art. This was a new experience for me, as I had very limited exposure to art growing up in London, given our school-holiday cultural treats were outings to the Museums of Imperial War and Natural History. They are magnificent in their own way, and the tyrannosaurus rex was certainly awe-inspiring, but it didn't qualify as great art, or serve as an entree into fine art. In Florence, however, even the walk down to the centre of the city on a blisteringly hot day meant passing multiple sculptures created by giants of the Renaissance period.

The city was steeped in history. For instance, the Ponte

Vecchio, which we needed to cross on our first day, translated as 'the old bridge', and it deserved its name. While this version of the bridge had been there in its current form since the sixteenth century, it had replaced bridges that dated back to the tenth century, before they were destroyed. And, being from the UK, I did understand 'old'. I had attended school and spent most of my adolescent and adult life in and around a town called Pinner. That town traced its heritage back to the fourteenth century at least, with a fair still taking over the main streets once a year, since licence was granted in 1336 by King Edward III. This walk in Florence, though, was like stepping back in time, past the old shops on the existing bridge, with their heavy wood and iron shutters. These shops had replaced the original butchers and fishmongers, when the smell from those premises had become too great for the delicate noses of the medieval aristocrats, who used the bridge to travel to the city centre. Living in medieval times, they would have been used to some rancid city smells, so the odours from the original shops must have been spectacularly bad.

There was one other intriguing element to the bridge and this part of the town – the Vasari Corridor, which is an elevated and totally enclosed passage, which connects the Palazzo Pitti to the Uffizi Gallery – that well-known Aladdin's cave for art lovers, and one which we hoped to visit at some stage during our stay. The elevated corridor had been built at the request of the Medici family, so they wouldn't have to mingle with the people of Florence, who they ruled.

As we battled the large crowds ourselves, on our way into the city, I remarked to Jenny, 'If Florence was half as busy in the Medici's time, frankly I don't blame them for wanting their own passage!'

Once we were clear of the busy throng, we headed to the flea and straw markets, to investigate shopping targets for Jenny, but found they were even busier than the bridge. So we navigated our way to the Amex office for phone calls and letters, and then found a place to buy fruit and veggies for our healthy dinner that night. As we were still in the city centre later in the afternoon, we did notice that the usually busy *duomo* was relatively quiet, so we popped in for a quick tour of the cathedral. The outside is famously made of pink, green and white marble so has a unique look to it, but when we went inside, we were a little disappointed. Clearly, we had been saturated with medieval monuments over the last months, raising our expectations. While the grandeur of the soaring ceilings and architraves was impressive, especially given the date of the building, in the Middle Ages, the beauty seemed to us to be on the outside rather than inside.

The following day we were still recovering from our long, hot ride and so we had a lie-in and a sluggish start. However, as we were heading past the Piazzale Michelangelo, my heart rate briefly shot up. A blur of movement off to my left was chasing a lizard across the path and, as it did so, it shot straight between my feet.

'Shit, it's a snake!' I shouted, stating the bleeding obvious and hopping from foot to foot.

Jenny, who had been following me, and a young couple who were walking towards us, had all seen me jumping around and they were demonstrating a distinct lack of sympathy – I could tell because of the peals of laughter coming from both directions.

In my defence, I had been programmed to react quickly to snakes, when I'd lived in Australia. I had been helping to clear the undergrowth in a friend's Sydney backyard and we had both jumped a mile in the air when we saw a brown snake slithering for cover, after my fellow gardener had destroyed its resting place. Recovering from that scare afterwards in the local pub, we were told by a grizzled Aussie who was propping up the bar, that the snake was probably more scared of us than we were of it. 'Frankly, I find that quite hard to believe!' my friend had pointedly told him. Especially given that, as English working tourists, we had taken the trouble to discover which animals in Australia were deadly, and we had known that brown snakes were definitely in that category. The national broadcaster had also helpfully explained one evening on TV that, '… an untreated eastern brown snake bite can kill in under half an hour. It's arguably the quickest killing venom in the world.'

So, my reaction on that footpath in Florence was not totally without context. But I could see Jenny and the young couple's point, as this was quite a small snake and was unlikely to be venomous. Oh well, my reflexes and my agility seemed to be pretty good.

Once my heart rate had returned to double figures, we continued on our way to the Academy of Fine Arts. Unfortunately it was closed, so we meandered past the Uffizi to check out the queues, which were long; after that we went 'down market' for lunch, with a shared pizza and *malaga* ice cream. We ate it while sitting on the stone benches around the Piazza della Signoria, soaking up the historic setting. I was loving the way you could just grab a tasty slice of pizza and an ice cream for a snack on the move, as opposed to the ubiquitous sausage roll and sugary doughnuts you might find in a typical English high street. The joy of travel – one person's 'normal' is someone else's 'special'.

We were late back to the camp site, so cooking wasn't high on our list of priorities and the camp shop had some two litre bottles of Chianti Bianco. Having selected this classic Italian wine, we decided to pair it with some food worthy of the vintage … so we went with an extra-large bag of salt and vinegar crisps. As I said to Jenny at the time, 'With this wine, we should be less worried about choosing food that will bring out the subtlety of the grape and more concerned with providing some lining for our stomachs.'

We made a valiant attempt to finish it, but only managed to polish off half the bottle, so we adjourned to our tent and nodded off rather quickly.

Despite our alcoholic end to the day, we rose early, but then we stopped to chat to a couple of fellow cycle tourists – our Kiwi pal from Pisa and a French Canadian. By the time we had each finished sharing stories of mountains climbed, punctures suffered, and locals encountered, it was starting to sound a little like the classic *Monty Python* Yorkshiremen sketch, with escalating levels of hardship, though we didn't think we could compete with John the Kiwi, who had ridden over the Alps. So, we trotted down to the centre to pick up lunch and gather our strength for what was supposed to be a day of shopping and negotiating for some leather goods in the markets of Florence.

Things were starting to get serious for Jenny, I could tell, and frankly I was glad to have her eye for fashion with me as we plunged into the fray. Like many young men of my vintage, shopping had always been more of a necessity, although in the late 1970s and early eighties there were some very questionable choices being made across the board, at least in the UK. For instance, I have no idea in retrospect why men of a certain age, typically with *Magnum P.I.*-style moustaches, thought it was cool to wear velvet-looking 'warm up suits', whatever they were. Or why women wore jackets with shoulders too big to comfortably walk through doors. Mind you, many of my acquaintances in the early 1980s were busy wearing what looked like puffy-sleeved pirate shirts, accessorised with bandanas around their necks, aping the latest chart sensation on *Top of the Pops*. So, no-one was covering themselves in glory in the fashion stakes.

But back in Florence we both had our eyes on leather bomber jackets, and I had a credible fashion advisor, so I was prepared to take the plunge. Leather being an expensive commodity in the UK, I'd never owned one, but it seemed that in Florence, bargains could be had. Guided by the much more experienced shopping eye of my cycling companion, we bought a shirt, jumper, and leather jacket for me, for less than the price of one leather jacket in London, and the material in Italy was higher quality. However, Jenny reserved the professional negotiating skills for her own purchase and secured a beautiful suede jacket for less than the Italian lire equivalent of twenty-eight pounds sterling – now that was impressive shopping.

Later that day, I wasn't sure whether it was the excitement of the negotiations, or Jenny's under-reported allergy to major world cities, but she was feeling decidedly unwell again. It did coincide with my serving a large plate of bolognaise, which I had slaved over for half an hour. But she assured me that it wasn't a reflection on my culinary skills, and I was therefore doing my best not to take it personally. Poor Jenny. I ended up eating both portions and she managed to keep a little tea and plain food down before we headed off to our sloping tent pitch for the night.

The following day we had struck the weekend and so the locals were well and truly out in force, which made the town even more lively and vibrant. We wandered down to the train station to consider our upcoming travel plans – we were hoping to send our bikes over the Alps to Freiburg and then catch a train ourselves down to Rome, up to Venice and through Switzerland. I had a feeling it was not going to be straightforward, especially when discussions would be in Italian, but we would find out on Monday when we attempted to negotiate our way through the various options. Then it was back into the markets where, buoyed by her success of the previous day, and lured by the mind-boggling variety of goods for sale, Jenny dived in again and found a pair of shoes and various presents for her family and friends.

We then thought a change of pace might be good, so we wandered into the main square, which was jumping with people and crowded with scores of caricature artists, who had set up their easels and were doing a brisk trade. We stopped to watch one of the artists, who seemed a little gentler with his subjects than others, and decided we would give it a try. The act of sitting for a portrait, even a caricature, was not very difficult. However, being an Englishman and therefore almost biologically programmed to avoid public displays or showiness, it was quite nerve-racking. Largely because scores of mostly American tourists stood behind the caricature artist, looking at each of us in turn and offering opinions such as:

'Look at the shape of that guy's ears in the drawing.'

'I don't think his nose is that big in real life.'

Or, 'Oh look, he's drawn a really short skirt on that girl!'

When he had finished, though, we both thought he managed a good balance of humour and accuracy, capturing faces, attributes and mannerisms in the drawing as well, which I guess is the mark of a good caricature artist. We were happy to pay the 5,000 lire to be able to take them away with us, and we still have them today. We finished the day with our two cycling tourist buddies back in the camp site, where they generously helped us finish our mega bottle of Chianti, sparing us another early morning headache in the process.

It was still stiflingly hot and very humid when the next day dawned, which I presumed was because Florence is a fair way south and built in a bowl-like indentation in the river valley. So, we showered and headed down very early, in an attempt to beat the hordes of people we expected would show up for the free entry at the Uffizi Gallery. Belatedly we splashed out for a city guide that included the Uffizi, and in retrospect, it would have been helpful to have had from day one – oh well, we'd know to look out for similar guides in Rome and Venice. We were not the only people with the idea of getting into the Uffizi early though, and the crowd was already large an hour before they opened.

I was watching some of the tourists, who I assumed were English as they were pointlessly trying to form a queue. We had been in the country long enough to know that, when the doors opened, this was going to be an exercise in futility, so we deployed our recently learned techniques – which involved me saying, '*Mi scusi*' loudly, while avoiding the dagger-like glances of other tourists, and ghosting through gaps with Jenny in my slipstream. It was just like being back on the rugby pitch, but without the need for as much liniment or physical contact. Also, I wasn't doing the English reputation any harm, as people still mostly assumed that I was a Northern German.

When we made it into the Uffizi it was a bit of a bun fight to get around, with a combination of locals and tourists jostling for views. Fortunately for me, the majority of the other people in the rooms were well below my eye-line, so I was able to see a lot more than would otherwise have been possible and could clear a path for Jenny to see as well. As a novice in the art world, I was mostly following Jenny who knew which artists she was keen to view. I could tell she was like a kid in a sweetshop, as she saw 'in the flesh' some of the original paintings by artists that, until that point, she had only seen in books. I was personally struck by some of the more dramatic and large canvasses, especially those by Rubens, which were in the final gallery – the largest was probably 30 by 15 feet and it took an age to even grasp what was on the canvas, let alone the detail of the brushstrokes and technique. It was impossible to do justice to the range of great masters that were exhibited. We spent time looking at Botticellis, inevitably Michelangelos, Rembrandts (which were a little dark for my taste, to be honest), and a surprise in Caravaggio, whose *Sacrifice of Isaac* had both Jenny and me spellbound. The guide declared, quite justifiably, that, 'the Uffizi Gallery has the most exclusive collection of paintings in Europe'. This would be a place to return to again and again, I imagined, and well done to the Florentines, who made it free to anyone who wanted to go every Sunday.

Sated by our exposure to so many great works of art and artists, we were surprised later in the day by an entirely less cultural but still entertaining spectacle. From our perch above the bowl of Florence, we were treated, along with the rest of the populace, to a one-hour fireworks display. They were launching most of the fireworks from the Piazzale Michelangelo, which was only 200 metres from our camp site, so we had front row seats. We could tell the locals enjoyed it as well because it was accompanied by a virtually nonstop cacophony of scooter and car horns every time there was a particularly spectacular rocket or colourful pyrotechnic display. We drank quite a bit more wine with our Kiwi pal, swapped addresses, and retired to our sloping sleeping quarters, ready to do battle with the train staff in the morning.

We were still really enjoying Florence, but we did need to get organised for our next leg, which seemed like it might involve some serious logistical skills. Having cleaned our bikes and ourselves, we made for the train station to see what would be possible. We were immediately reminded why we had chosen to cycle – for the simplicity and also the cost factors. We started our discussions at the train station, where we were told we would need a ticket to register the bikes. So, we went to a freight agent, whose only option was to send them express, and we could almost have bought a new bike for the eye-watering cost. We then returned to Transalpino, who were the agent most travellers used to move around Europe. We secured two tickets to Freiburg, via Bologna and Verona, from where we understood we could get a train to and from Venice. Finally, we bought tickets to Rome one way.

This was elaborate and quite expensive, but we weren't going to be physically capable of riding our bikes with all our gear over the Alps, nor did we have the time or money for that extended trip. So, this would be the best option to ensure we could spend time in two much anticipated cities, Rome and Venice, and still cycle further north in Europe, when we caught up with our bikes. Having consigned our faithful transport to the tender care of the Italian rail service, we grabbed some pizza and caught a bus back to the camp, where we finished our washing and lay around in the sun writing postcards after five hectic days of sightseeing, in our first real major city since Paris.

CHAPTER 8
Roma and Venezia

Before departing Florence, I was pleasantly surprised when we went to settle our bill in the camp site, to find they only planned to charge us for six rather than the seven nights we had spent in their grounds. I did wonder whether it was because our pitch had been on a slope – one which discouraged tossing and turning in our sleep, in case we gathered momentum like a mini-avalanche and carved a swathe through the other tents on our way into the city centre. The duty manager was trying to explain something to me, but given his English was non-existent and our Italian was still patchy, I figured if he was happy then so were we. Having eventually left our home for the last seven days and made our way to the train station, we did have to clear a passage through several extended families to get onto the train to Rome. Once on board, and with what we assumed were the loud best wishes ringing in our ears from the still-gesticulating families on the platform, we secured two seats for the entire three-hour journey in a second-class cabin. We also crammed in our panniers, tent and other material and, from the looks on the faces of the locals already on the train, we didn't need to be told how they felt – they were clearly thrilled to have us as travelling companions.

As we started off, we were also being treated to a very loud, though seemingly friendly conversation from the cabin next door. It all sounded quite good-natured, but as a conservative Englishman brought up to always 'speak quietly in public', I did think the volume was verging on being rude. But then again, if I compare that experience to the type of conversations to which we're often inadvertently subjected in the *digital age*, it was nothing. Fortunately, the noise from our relatively loud fellow travellers mercifully abated quickly, so we could snooze. We also arrived physically rested, having avoided cycling any of the numerous hills we saw on the way to Rome, which was a pleasant change. Although, we did make up for it as we negotiated the public transport, taking a bus and Metro ride while carrying all our panniers and gear, on our way to the camping ground on the northern outskirts of the city.

It was late afternoon by the time we arrived, slightly the worse for wear. So, we quickly assembled our tent and bought a guidebook of Rome, which had some very useful suggested itineraries, and the same sort of detail we had latterly stumbled across and benefitted from in Florence. We then treated ourselves to a leisurely sit-down meal with house Chianti and decided on a couple of itineraries for the next day. I was excited to be in Rome – I had always been fascinated by the Roman Empire, so exploring the remaining relics, such as the Colosseum, Catacombs, and Forum, was going to be a major highlight, as it probably is for many people. We finished our meal with ice cream from the local *gelateria* before an early night, although it was proving harder than anticipated to nod off as we lay there talking about our plans for the following day in the Eternal City – we felt a little like kids again on the night before Christmas, when the morning couldn't come fast enough.

'Well, this is an unexpected treat,' I said to Jenny, as we polished off our cereal and fresh milk the next day for breakfast. I had been happy to eat like a local most days, although I guess you can take the boy out of Britain, but you can't take Britain out of the boy – we had discovered a small cereal aisle at the camp site store. Clearly, they accommodated a lot of Brits there. Two bowls of Weetabix later and we headed off into town, via six different buses, each at 400 lire a pop – this was looking like an expensive city. We made it to our initial destination of the Piazza di Spagna and dropped into the Amex office for our mail, which yielded a mix of birthday cards and letters for each of us – so we were both happy and back in contact, albeit briefly.

We then set off on our first itinerary and went straight to the Trevi Fountain, which was predictably attracting quite a few other tourists – not surprising as it had been immortalised in at least two Hollywood movies and arguably, most famously in, Federico Fellini's La Dolce Vita. While the actual fountain had been providing water to the baths and the fountains of central Rome at the height of their empire, the latest incarnation was only built in the eighteenth century, courtesy of a commission from then Pope Clemens XII. It was said that Alessandro Galilei, an architect from the same family as the famous astronomer Galileo, originally won the commission for the project but it was ultimately given to a native Roman architect called Nicola Salvi after a Roman public outcry. The reason for the public's objections? Galilei was a Florentine and that just wouldn't do for the proud Roman populace. The current version was indeed very impressive, reaching a height of 85 feet and made from travertine stone, the same material as the Colosseum. It was well known as a place for tourists and locals alike to stand and throw coins over their shoulders into the water, hoping to receive some good luck from the associated wishes. We threw in our obligatory coins, although our wishes were not very lofty at that stage, being a combination of good weather and easy riding conditions.

Our next stop was the Piazza Venezia and the towering, and very white, Altare della Patria, or Altar of the Nation (Fatherland), as we understood it to mean. As we approached the Piazza, this enormous and somewhat overpowering building dominated the skyline. We heard from listening to one of the guided tours, that there was controversy there too, as there seemed to be with many Roman monuments. This time it was not about the person selected to design it, but rather the choice of building material – white marble instead of travertine, with which the Eternal City had always been built.

Apparently, travertine absorbs the sun's rays, which in an almost perpetually hot city like Rome, seemed like a good plan. Whereas marble does the opposite, and the ever-vigilant city population felt the resulting glare overpowered nearby Roman monuments, and was totally out of context. As a Londoner, I could certainly understand this desire to preserve both the look and feel of the ancient city for which they were custodians. I'm not sure I would have appreciated someone coming along and building an ugly monument within spitting distance of, say, the Tower of London. And, maybe that sun *was* bouncing off the marble statue into the eyes of the Italian motorists, because one of them nearly collected me, as I tried to cross the busy thoroughfare to get closer for a better photo. As with my previous close calls with Italian drivers, I was going to assume that the general arm-waving and calling out as they swerved past me were good wishes and a hearty welcome to their town, so I returned the compliment in kind, 'Thank you, my good man, it's a pleasure to be here!'

There, I was sure that was appreciated. Jenny just shook her head and rolled her eyes at me, but then that was not an uncommon reaction.

As you do in Rome, we then wandered past the 2,000-year-old Forum and a statue of Julius Caesar on our way to the Colosseum. We had to pause as we approached this ancient structure, because nothing really prepared us for the sheer scale when we saw it in person. Even in its partly crumbled state, it is extraordinarily impressive, appearing to rise almost out of the stone of the surrounding streets.

I was a little awe-struck and as I said to Jenny, 'If it has that effect on us in the twentieth century, imagine the impact on the poor souls who were being brought to Rome, to play a part in the so-called games!'

Our guidebook informed us that it was 620 by 513 feet, and when it was at the height of its use, it could seat up to 50,000 people. It even had a series of awnings rigged from large poles set into the top tier, which were operated by hundreds of sailors to keep the patrons out of the intense sun. The design and engineering of the freestanding structure was incredible and would have put some twentieth century architects to shame. The main structural framework and facade were made from travertine, the secondary walls from volcanic tufa, and the inner bowl and the arcade vaults from concrete. I was guessing they had quite a large building budget, and of course an unending supply of free labour from the slave markets, but even so it was impressive.

The arena's surface was no longer in place, having originally been made of wood, but that meant we could see all the way down into the cells and rooms where prisoners and gladiators would be housed, near to the wild animals that would occasionally be used to torment them. The surface during the Roman Empire was apparently covered with sand and hosted everything from hand-to-hand gladiatorial combat, the slaughter of innocents by men and wild animals, to large-scale land and naval battles – all of which took place in front of big, enthusiastic Roman crowds. We could easily have stayed for much longer, letting our imaginations run wild and reliving scenes from *Ben Hur*, but we wanted to make it to the Catacombs of San Sebastiano before it became too dark.

We didn't have much time there, but did manage to squeeze in a forty-five-minute guided tour of that ancient burial chamber for early Christians. It was easy to become blasé in Rome, given the abundance of historical monuments and locations in the city, but walking around Rome was fascinating and a genuinely educational experience. I hadn't realised, for instance, that Italy had been a united country for less than two hundred years – even though Rome was founded in 753 BC, fully seven hundred years before the Romans made it the centre of their empire. Coming from the UK and with London as my comparator, I had wrongly assumed that Italy was united much earlier. As I thought about the powerful trading regions of Venice, Rome, Florence, Milan and Genoa, which had sprung out of Italy during the Middle Ages, I realised that some of them were more powerful than other nations. No surprise then that national unification had not been on the agenda until some of those fortunes had started to wane in more recent history.

Anyway, we were running out of daylight and, after one unsuccessful attempt, we managed to find the right bus to take us back to the Colosseum, from where we needed to catch two more connections to arrive at our camp site. Up until Rome, we hadn't needed to engage with public transport in Italy, apart from the train journey from Florence, but our bus rides in Rome were collectively one of the 'hairier' experiences on our trip. Not only did the cars hurtle around the roads like dodgem cars at your favourite fun park, but the bus drivers that we experienced threw their long and articulated vehicles around corners and between lanes as if they were riding a Vespa on a racetrack. You had to hang on to something or someone to avoid bouncing off the sides and into fellow passengers.

Having recovered from our wild rides of the previous day, we were up at the crack of dawn again and Jenny was keen to ensure the day went well.

'Right, we need to dress "decently" today,' she told me.

I was initially concerned that she had decided overnight that we had been dressing indecently on the trip to date and, if we had possessed a mirror, I would have been checking myself for signs of this oversight. However, it turned out she was talking about the requirements at Saint Peter's Basilica, in the Vatican City. Apparently, based on her insights from her previous trip to Rome, and the advice from our friendly guidebook, she knew that women were not allowed to have bare shoulders or short dresses and men could not wear shorts. So, she pulled her skirt down to her hips and covered her shoulders, while I dug out my only pair of long trousers for the occasion. It was good advice because sure enough, at the steps of the church, young men and women were being regularly turned away for being incorrectly dressed, by three or four officious-looking priests.

As we arrived in the square of St Peter's, like most people, we were impressed by its scale and structure. Although when you got close up it was clearly being affected by the same pollution that afflicted all monuments in major capital cities. However, the real treasures were inside, and we were immediately bombarded by history and grandeur, walking through the Vatican Museum, Hall of Sculptures and Hall of Maps. It was the Sistine Chapel that everyone really came to see, though. When we managed to shuffle inside that hallowed space, we joined the hundred-plus throng of people, moving slowly through the open area in a ragged circle, looking upwards and anywhere except where they were going.

The ceiling and far walls are breathtaking, in terms of both their scale and the volume of detail achieved by Michelangelo and his team of assistants. But time was limited in the chapel, so we were only in there for thirty minutes and, with so much detail crammed onto every available surface, it was not possible to absorb everything. We concentrated, therefore, on the end wall and the representation of the creation of Adam. This was allegedly the first attempt to show God as an actual figure, with the now classical old-man-and-flowing-beard appearance, so it was quite controversial for its time. Before this, God had mostly been depicted in paintings as a hand appearing from above. We could tell that many of the visitors were practising Christians, from their gestures and from overhearing their mumbled litanies. But even if you weren't, you had to be grateful it had been so well preserved, and we were left awe-struck at the achievement. The entrance fee of 5,000 lire was the best value Italian tourist location in our time there.

Providing the opposite in terms of value was the classically unimpressive food that was being served in what passed for a snack bar after we exited the Sistine Chapel, and before leaving the precinct. As I looked at my plastic food at fine-dining prices, I wasn't even sure how to describe it. Something that had never been a problem to date in Italy and our first disappointing meal of the trip.

'I think I understand one of the reasons the Catholic Church isn't short of a few bob,' I said to Jenny. 'I feel like I've just wandered into a 1970s British Rail canteen – cheap food, at high prices!'

Following the unfortunate juxtaposition of the Sistine Chapel high point and the cafe's culinary low point, we took another couple of bus-come-dodgem-car rides back to the camp site, where we attempted to rebalance our equilibriums after the midday 'snack', with a healthy bowl of fresh fruit, accompanied by yoghurt and fresh milk.

The next day we had a late train booked to take us to Venice, but the camp site manager kindly let us leave our gear on site while I went looking for a bank to change some money, in the local suburb on the outskirts of Rome. On arrival it became clear that the Italians did indeed have their own version of the unhelpful customer service agent, as I was shuffled from one area to another and finally to the end of a 'queue' of around twenty-five loudly complaining Italians. I figured, if they weren't getting satisfaction then I had no chance – even if I managed to negotiate my way to the front of the crowd. So, I retreated to the camp site where

Jenny was able to effortlessly change money for virtually the same rate, once she had sweet-talked them into not charging her commission. Clearly, we had been sending the wrong person in to change money in Italy. With plenty of time left before we needed to leave, we chilled and lay around in the sun for four or five hours until it was time to pack our bags and exit the site.

But Rome wasn't finished with us yet, especially those bus drivers. When our bus drew up at the stop, Jenny climbed aboard, but as usual, the bus hadn't really stopped completely. So, as I had one foot on the entry platform, the driver tried to close the door and started moving off again. That was tricky, because I still had my remaining foot on the pavement, along with four panniers in my hands, so I was literally hopping along trying to keep up as he accelerated. The passengers nearest to the back of the bus noticed and shouted for the driver to stop, but he either didn't hear or took no notice.

So, stuck in the door and not wanting to hop all the way to the next stop, I yelled at the top of my voice, 'Hey, stop the bus!'

Jen said later that it was probably louder than I had intended, but I think I was venting my anger at all the bus drivers in Rome at the same time. Regardless, it had the desired effect, and he stopped the bus completely, opened the doors and allowed me to properly board. The other passengers were smiling at us; however, the bus driver was clearly not happy – maybe he was having a bad day? Either way, his driving deteriorated as we drew closer to the centre of Rome and all the passengers were forced to either cling to railings along the inside of the bus or hang onto a nearby strap, to avoid being thrown off their feet – even the locals started shouting at him at one point. He certainly wasn't hanging around and, as we were approaching the centre of town, I remember looking out of the window and catching Jenny's attention.

'Have you noticed there are two lanes of fast-moving traffic on our left and another two on our right?' I asked her.

'Yes, I have … why?' she said.

'Well, this is only a four-lane highway.'

I did feel sorry for the older and less nimble people in Rome who were forced to catch buses, because we were struggling to stay upright some of the time. I didn't think they would fare well with buses that slowed down to a partial halt, rather than coming to a complete stop, and then threw them around like rag dolls when they sped up again. It seemed somewhat 'Darwinian' and I was a little surprised there were so many surviving, older people in Rome.

Having negotiated our last bus in Rome, we lugged our gear to the train station, where we gratefully slumped into a couple of chairs in the booking office hall and settled in for a three-to-four hour wait for our train. We'd arrived earlier than planned, but we'd learnt during our brief stay in Rome that public transport could be quite unreliable. So, it was always best to allow plenty of time to compensate and we didn't want to miss our train. As we took in our surroundings, we were surprised to see a large number of what appeared to be homeless people, mostly with bottles of alcohol in their hands, wandering around the station. We'd only been there a few minutes when a young girl, who was also waiting for a train, came over to ask if she could wait with us. She was from Singapore, was travelling alone to Nice, and didn't really like the idea of waiting there by herself. Not only because of the wandering drunks, but also because of her experience as a young, non-Italian female in Rome, where she had been constantly 'approached' by young Italian men trying to hit on her. Based on what I had observed travelling with Jenny, including her bottom-pinching episode in a much smaller town, I was not entirely surprised to hear that. We were happy to let her sit with us and glad we talked with her in the end, because she had seen a timetable that told us our train was coming in earlier than expected. Hers was almost there as well, so we parted ways, narrowly making our connection.

We found a compartment that seemed to have sprung from the pages of an Italian film script, being occupied by a smiling nun in full habit and an older man in a beautifully tailored double-breasted suit, sporting a thin moustache and slicked back hair. The man made a show of offering Jenny his seat opposite the nun, with a flourish. That was kind of him, as it allowed us to collapse onto one bench seat and settle in for the ride to Bologna, where we would need to connect again. Jenny had promised me that she couldn't sleep on trains so would keep me company, but her head was resting on my shoulder, and she was asleep almost straight after leaving the station, all the way to Bologna. Fortunately, the ticket office was open when we arrived at 3:30 am and we were able to buy a ticket to Mestre, which is the mainland town for Venice, arriving just after 8 am. On arriving, we tried phoning one recommended camp site, which didn't seem to exist. Then, just as I was thinking that the AA had given up when they got this far into Italy, they were recommending camp sites again and had clearly decided this part of Italy warranted some attention. They cheerfully informed us that there was an option where, 'The site lies on meadowland scattered with poplars.'

After I phoned that site, we had directions and were soon on our way, on 'Bus number 3 to Camping Jolly'. Let's hope it is, I thought.

After the public transport challenges of Rome, we were delighted to discover that we only needed to take one bus, which actually stopped at the allotted place to let us off, followed by a kilometre walk to reach the recommended camp site. It was very pleasant, sitting on the edge of a large lake and with substantial shade provided by the promised poplars. Because our connections had all surprisingly worked, we were in the site and with our tent ready to go by 9:30 am. While we were certainly weary after travelling all night, we weren't sleepy and we were both very excited at the prospect of seeing Venice for the first time – so we showered, ate and then found a bus to Venice to have a walk around.

This would be our fourth major city in Europe on this trip, and it was our third in Italy, but Venice was well known as a city like no other. For a start, it was built on more than one-hundred small islands in a lagoon in the Adriatic Sea. It had no roads, and people moved around by walking on footpaths, across the more than 400 bridges, or by boat on one of the 170-plus canals. I wasn't sure why you would build in such a location, but when the early settlers had made the decision to build there, they had drained areas of the lagoon, dug canals and reinforced the banks with thousands of large tree trunks, driven into the silt and mud, as piles. They then proceeded to lay wooden platforms and stone on top of those piles, which were the foundations for building the city. I'm sure that made sense at the time, but more recently this design had been proving problematic, because Venice was sinking at the rate of one-to-two millimetres a year. When compared to the waterlines on paintings by the renowned Venetian artist Canaletto, tides at the time of our visit were lapping on average 30 inches higher than when he was painting in the eighteenth century. Even since the start of the twentieth century, marble steps that had once led down to the waterline were now completely submerged except at very low tide. Despite all of this, and the infamous smell that we were experiencing on a warm summer's day, it was still a city we both very much wanted to explore, and we were delighted to be there.

We arrived in Piazzale Roma, which is a square on the island of Venice close to the only bridge from the mainland, Ponte della Libertà. We had learnt from our time in Florence and Rome, and had purchased a similarly useful guidebook that morning, although this one had been printed in 1981. That didn't seem to be a problem, as buildings hadn't changed there much in the last century, let alone the last three years. However, prices had changed, apparently. The book informed us that we needed to pay 500 lire for the boat trip. When we bought our bus tickets, we had noticed that the same company sold tickets for the buses and the boats, and those same tickets had photos of buses *and* boats boldly displayed. So, we assumed the one ticket covered both trips.

In fact, as we found out afterwards, they were separate and the boat trip along the Grand Canal was either 1,200 or 1,500 lire, depending on the boat you chose. Oops! Fortunately, the ticket collectors in Venice weren't very thorough and no-one checked our ticket, so we had rather a cheap tour on the first day. On our free boat trip, we noticed that the Grand Canal was very busy with many of the 300-odd gondolas that plied their trade in Venice and many larger tourist boats crisscrossing in apparent chaos. As two people who had experienced the random traffic movement of motorists along the French and Italian Rivieras, it all felt quite normal, though, with the added benefit that, as a pedestrian or boat passenger, you were unlikely to be run down along the way.

'Have you noticed the Middle Eastern look of some of these buildings?' Jenny remarked, as we were slowly cruising past on our boat on the Grand Canal.

I hadn't, but when she pointed out the Byzantine mosaics on various facades it became obvious. Given its trading heritage, those early Venetian traders had brought more than merely silks and spices – they had also brought Byzantine and Islamic influences, which found their way into the blend of architecture that now defined Venice. Walking around, we were also intrigued by the variety of shops, many of which appeared to be focused purely on selling goods to tourists, especially the mask shops. And the Venetians took their mask-wearing seriously. Apparently that tradition, back in the seventeenth century, had only been allowed during the annual carnival and anyone who broke that edict was punished with up to two years in prison, or a public beating at the 'pillar of shame'. Clearly those early Venetians didn't want you hiding your face around town when there was no carnival underway! We were feeling a little weary by that stage, so headed back to the camp site, with a bit of unwanted additional exercise, having alighted at the wrong stop and walked an extra two kilometres around suburban Marghera to our camp site, where we rustled up our go-to spag bol before heading off for our first proper sleep in forty-eight hours.

We slept very soundly, although when I woke, I was greeted initially by laughter and then a look of concern. 'What were you doing last night?' Jenny wanted to know. 'You look like you've just come off a rugby pitch!'

When she pulled out her small mirror to show me, I

realised my mouth was quite swollen and that, either Jenny had accidentally struck me in her sleep while turning over, or I had been bitten on the inside of my top lip by a mosquito. More likely to be the latter, we thought. In current parlance, imagine a botox injection that didn't go well, and you'll get the picture – and there are plenty of those around! Anyway, it seemed that someone, who would remain nameless, went for a nocturnal trip and left the zip of the inner tent open. Not normally a problem, except we were camped beside a very large body of still water, and it was humid, so there were plenty of mozzies around, one of which had invited itself into our tent.

'If only that had happened in France,' I replied. 'I could have passed for a local, with an exaggerated Gallic pout!'

Despite being unable to eat properly while I waited for the swelling to go down, we eventually got our act together and staggered off to the bus stop. But the day was very humid, and we were still tired from the missing night's sleep on our train trip to Mestre. So, after we had been waiting for some time for a bus that didn't seem to be coming, we decided to turn tail and head back to our camp. We spent the day lying around in the shade, chatting to a couple of Aussie sheep farmers who were doing their grand European tour, before cooking a bland meal of ravioli, spices and onions – we were certainly living the high life in Venice! Now, of course, the mosquitos had well and truly become aware of our presence – well *my* presence. Jenny still didn't seem to be attacked by them at all. So, before bed I reprised my 'dance of the mosquitos', as I chased them around the inside of our tent before sleep, so I wouldn't suffer the same fate again overnight.

We had big plans for the next day, so we woke early to catch a bus and then walk from Piazzale Roma to San Marco. It was cheaper than the boat trip and was an interesting walk, which took us along small streets, gave us views to the Grand Canal around almost every corner, and guided us across multiple little bridges and side canals. The signposting to San Marco was good, which was fortunate, because if we had tried to follow the numbering we would have been completely lost – houses in Venice were numbered according to districts, not streets. I expect even the postmen struggled. We made it to the main square by 11 am and were just in time to hear the single remaining bell in the tower of Saint Mark's Campanile, on the corner of the square, strike the time. Before the bell tower collapsed in 1902 and was then rebuilt, there used to be five bells, each of which had a different purpose – calling the lords to assemble, announcing senate meetings, marking midday, telling the local craftsmen to begin or cease working, and announcing an execution. Now, the remaining large bell marked each hour for the locals and tourists and was attended by two bronze Moor figures, who alternately struck the bell with large hammers. I imagined that it was much less noisy and less confusing for the locals than when five different bells were regularly going off in the tower – you'd certainly want to make sure you turned up for the correct bell… and I also expect they were generally pleased to be spared the 'execution' bell.

On the way back we realised that, while the signposting was good, it only went one way, so we had to follow our noses and became lost a few times, wandering over small private bridges that seemed to end at someone's front door. Despite these detours, we eventually found Piazzale Roma, and Jenny was able to hunt for, and buy, some Murano glass objects. It was renowned as being very fine and virtually unbreakable and she eventually settled on two lovely necklaces, into which the craftsman had managed to fit red, blue, and green beads, flecked with gold and yellow.

This was our last day in Venice, so arriving back at our camp site, we quickly packed, ate and showered before heading off for our train to Bologna. When we arrived at Mestre the station was quiet, but I was spotted by a scruffy-looking young Englishman, who strolled over and proceeded to ask for some money for an ice cream. We donated a small sum, partially as an act of solidarity to a fellow countryman, but also to get rid of him, because as he moved closer we became aware that either the showers weren't working where he was staying, or he just couldn't be bothered washing. In that heat, either way, it wasn't pleasant!

We eventually left at around 9 pm, arriving at Bologna at just after 11 pm. We would have to wait four-and-a-half hours for our connection to Lucerne, which we had chosen because of its convenience as a direct connection point to Freiburg, our first German destination. Then the Italian train service gave us one last reminder of the 'directionally correct' nature of Italian timekeeping, when the train finally showed up an hour late. We gratefully climbed aboard and then had to wake a couple of sleeping backpackers, who had stretched out fully on our seats – which made us very popular. It was only three hours to Milan where we thought we needed to change, but when we disembarked, we discovered that some carriages would continue all the way to Lucerne without stopping, so we loaded ourselves and our gear into them and settled in for the remainder of the night.

The train journey was peaceful and, before leaving Italy and while our experiences were still current, I was reflecting on the Italians and our thoughts, having spent over a month in their company. We had certainly liked most of what we experienced and saw. In fact, it was hard to find anything to dislike about the Italians, not that we had been trying. Even considering the occasional caricatures of Italian men and women we had seen – frankly, you could find similar stereotypical versions of Brits or Aussies in London and Sydney, so they weren't 'Robinson Crusoe' in that regard.

There had certainly been a few experiences that might be described as mild annoyances – especially for a Brit who had the importance of social order drummed into him from a very early age. Such as their failure to grasp or seemingly have any interest in the basic principles of queueing; driving fast while gesticulating with both hands; not doing what you said you would, when you said you would do it; and speaking loudly in small public spaces. But I'm sure the Italians felt that there were many annoying traits in the average Brit or Aussie at the time, and those small issues were far outweighed by the warm hospitality we experienced, and the infectious joy for life they mostly exhibited. I think we could all do worse than practice one of their mantras, *Non ti preoccupare! Andrà tutto bene, vedrai*, which translated as: 'Don't worry. Everything will be fine, you'll see.'

That may not always have been true, but it certainly cut down a lot of the stress on the way, which was no bad thing. So, on balance, we had really warmed to the Italians, their way of life, and *il bel paese.* We would certainly plan to return at some point to refresh that acquaintance.

CHAPTER 9
Switzerland, Germany and up the Rhine

Other than sounding like the title of a bad *Carry On* movie, this was going to be a very different chapter of our trip. Largely because we were not cycling over the Alps, which given the challenge we had found crossing Passo del Bracco, was looking like a very good idea. As we crossed the Swiss border on our train, the scenery was indeed mountainous, as you would expect. It was also spectacular, with massive snow-capped mountain peaks, crystal clear lakes and small waterfalls everywhere. When we arrived in Lucerne, the earlier sunny blue skies had been exchanged for the more familiar dark grey palate, with low threatening clouds.

'Looks like our usual riding weather,' I said to Jenny. 'It's about to rain!'

But, as we didn't have our bikes and didn't need to cycle anywhere, of course it stayed dry.

The differences between Italy and Switzerland could not have been more obviously demonstrated than during our first few hours in the country – the information bureau had maps and could explain them to us in English; the moneychanger at the bank was at the correct counter; I wasn't shunted from counter to counter randomly; and everyone was queueing. However, it was the bus ride to the camp site that provided the biggest contrast between the order-loving Swiss and the more freewheeling Italians. Inside the bus, there was an electronic route map that lit up when it was approaching the relevant stop, the driver called out the name before stopping and then he actually stopped to let people off. And finally, as I pointed out to Jenny: 'Have you noticed this road is three lanes wide and we only have one car either side of us?'

Not very remarkable, unless your last major bus ride and most recent reference point was on the four-lane racetrack that passed for a public freeway, heading into Rome. We also noticed that almost everyone we met spoke English. Except for the train station, where it would have been helpful for Jenny to use her German linguistic skills to help us secure lockers for two of our panniers. She was demonstrating some initial reluctance to speak German though, hiding behind me and pushing me forward to speak French when non-English language skills were required. Clearly, I was less concerned about making a fool of myself – must have been my years of practice?

In Lucerne, we were in the German part of Switzerland, having travelled through the Italian-speaking region on the way there and bypassing the French portion of the country to the west. No wonder many of the Swiss could easily switch from one language to another and that English was a common second language across the three areas – and my Canadian cousins told me they had it tough, because they needed two languages on all their packaging. Try telling that to the Swiss with three, plus near-universal English! When we arrived at our camp site it was clean, and we were able to machine wash our clothes for the first time since leaving home. We also figured that, as we had been conducting research diligently on the way through the rest of Europe, we needed to check out the famous Swiss products. So, we kicked that off with a very large bar of Swiss milk chocolate and local milk. We hadn't quite shaken Italy though, so spaghetti it was for dinner, followed by the remainder of the chocolate and milk – making sure we were working through the major food groups obviously.

We struggled awake the next day, as we had slept like proverbial logs, following our sleep deprived train trips of the last few days. And, moving on to the next of the famous Swiss food products, we decided that we needed to experience some classical Swiss muesli, which didn't disappoint, before venturing into Lucerne, which was a very pleasant thirty-minute stroll along a lake shore. The town dated from medieval times, which probably explained the long, winding bridge – the Kapellbrücke, or Chapel Bridge. It's a covered wooden footbridge spanning the river that flows into Lake Lucerne. We spent some time trying to decipher the engravings and carvings, but in the end, we decided they must be scenes from fables of some sort. Though, without the internet for reference back then and with no guidebook, we didn't know for sure.

Before we left home, we had been told that Switzerland was expensive and one look at the menu in a restaurant persuaded us that could well be true. It looked like our brief time in that town was going to be spent in supermarkets and then cooking at the camp site, as the prices were the most expensive we had seen since we had arrived in Europe. We also noticed that the vibe seemed quite relaxed – at odds with, yet maybe also because it was so well organised and ordered? It was so ordered, you could have been forgiven for wondering if you had wandered into a European version of *The Truman Show*, where everyone plays pre-ordained roles and no-one steps out of line or creates a fuss. It was certainly a very friendly town though and, as we were walking beside the almost impossibly clear lake, couples were strolling slowly, nodding and smiling to us as we passed.

The lake was picture-perfect and seemed like the perfect spot for lunch, so we found somewhere to buy dense Swiss bread, sausage meat and the ubiquitous *apfelstrudel.*

'I'm developing a real weakness for these,' I said to Jenny.

I have since found that there really is nothing that can replace a well-made apple strudel, especially when you're somewhere that takes the production seriously, such as the German part of Switzerland. Which was why I was having another later in the afternoon, because there were multiple options, and you should always be prepared to experience as many local varieties of the dominant cuisine as possible when travelling. Jenny's opting for a white Toblerone was also in the interests of research and because we had never seen one before – if there was anything that was quintessentially Swiss, Toblerone had to be it. Now I'm reflecting on our day, we did seem to be quite food-obsessed. Maybe it was because we didn't have to cycle and we could casually wander the streets, dipping into the local culinary treats at will. Although our early dinner of German *knockwurst* sausage and baked beans could hardly be listed among the gastronomic high points of the trip. That's why we finished the meal with a third helping of Swiss chocolate and fresh milk, before we wandered into town to see the city walls lit up, taking our leather jackets for a walk in the process, and grateful for the warmth they provided at that altitude. Not only did Lucerne put on a very pretty display, but impressively, the lights appeared exactly when advertised. The Swiss were nothing if not punctual.

The next day we were ready to head onwards and re-join our bikes, so we went back to the train station to reclaim our baggage. We were pleasantly surprised by a new experience, having only caught trains in the French and Italian Rivieras previously, which were a little more DIY in relation to moving baggage, and people, and … pretty well everything.

'Look at this,' I called out to Jenny, as she struggled up the platform under her load. 'There are luggage trolleys, they're free, and they work!'

It was amazing how simple organisational touches were surprising to us, after our time among the more free-wheeling Italians. However, we were both relieved as this was a very long train and, as we'd previously discovered in large towns without our bikes, our luggage was not designed to be toted around by hand for any distance. Whizzing up the platform on our new-found transport, we quickly located a carriage going all the way to our next destination, Freiberg, and in we climbed.

It was only a three-hour trip and the efficient German Customs boarded shortly after we passed through Basel, to check our papers. Bizarrely I felt nervous when I saw them, but then maybe I had watched too many war movies growing up as a teenager. As I confided quietly to Jenny, 'It always seemed to be on the train that the Allied POW escapee was tripped up, as he tried to speak German.'

She suggested that I should keep that particular line of thinking to myself, which was wise counsel, and now that she had to use her German, it was clearly good enough for me to remain quiet anyway. There was also a young Italian guy in our cabin whose papers were checked much more closely on a minicomputer, and who was then obliged to open all his bags, to be examined by the Customs official. He didn't seem phased and merely accepted it, looking at me and raising his eyebrows as if to say – This is just part of the process for a young Italian male heading into Germany.

As expected, we arrived on time in Freiberg. And let's face it, between the Germans and the Swiss, you couldn't find two countries who were more focused on order and timeliness anywhere on the planet. I was also reflecting as we crossed the border into Germany that, if there had been a longstanding history of conflict between the French and the British, then the relationship between the British and the Germans was much more complex. True, the British hadn't been conquered by them, as we had been by the French Normans in the Middle Ages – although it hadn't been for the lack of trying on behalf of the Germans in the twentieth century. The Germans had also made a fine art of breaking the hearts of generations of English football fans, by regularly knocking England out of the latter stages of major championships, with the notable exception of 1966.

Despite all of those reasons for a lingering enmity between the two countries, and the efforts of the same press that fed the xenophobic tendencies of the British towards the French – Britain and Germany were probably more like one another than any other European countries. They both liked order; were both regarded as being a little 'dour'; and both had quite dry senses of humour, even if the British pretended that the Germans didn't have one. In addition, the British monarchy was littered with German influences and, it seemed from our three months on the Continent, that I looked more German than some Germans – maybe we were closer than I had considered. Fortunately, Jenny experienced no such qualms as everyone loved the Aussies – even the Germans.

As tourists, we were happily adjusting to this more ordered existence and predictability. So, having found more of those efficient and free trolleys at Freiberg station, we headed for a bank to change some of our money into deutschmarks and pfennigs, just to be prepared. As we had sent our bikes from Florence before we headed south to Rome and Venice, we had not seen them for a few weeks and figured there must be some cost for leaving them with the authorities. But, to our pleasant surprise, they weren't going to charge us a pfennig.

'That's very nice of them,' Jenny said. 'They could easily have charged us for storing them and we would have been none the wiser.'

That was certainly true, so we pushed them out of the holding area before they could change their minds. They must have been there for seven or eight days, so our first impressions were lining up with our expectations for German efficiency. This was reinforced further when Jenny entered an information office and they had a free detailed map that we could take to guide our way to the camp site. Having loaded our panniers and reacquainted ourselves with our well-travelled machines, we wobbled off into a very new experience.

Fresh from our French and Italian road sharing adventures, where cars, buses and bikes existed in very close and sometimes scary proximity, this felt a little like a twilight world. We immediately found ourselves on a well signposted and separated bike path, which even had a kerb, marking the path for bikes and pedestrians, and our very own bicycle traffic lights. We'd never seen anything like that in 1984; the UK and Australia certainly weren't that enlightened. It seemed the Germans definitely deserved their reputation for orderliness and efficiency. With such an easy riding environment, we were able to look at the map regularly and found our camp site with no trouble. It was very clean, well laid out and they had a washing machine and hot showers. This seemed perfect, although I think the camp site manager probably wondered who these strange cycle tourists were when I asked him how much they charged for the use of the aforementioned hot showers. Clearly, we were heading back into more reasonable territory, although somewhat surprisingly, the camp site was cheaper than those in Italy – a place we had expected to be the cheapest. The food and beer were definitely cheap in Germany, and the beer had a very good reputation, so we loaded up with eight reasonably priced bottles of pilsner, at the equivalent of two pounds twenty-five for the lot, plus our share of goodies for dinner. This definitely included many of the important food groups, containing, meat, grains, veggies, and of course dairy, represented by milk chocolate.

Freiberg was a very agreeable place from what we could tell on our first day. It's a university town, with quaint squares and cobbled streets, through which charming trams ran as main public transport. This did mean that those same streets were crisscrossed with tram tracks, which needed careful navigation, and required that the average cycle tourist stay alert. However, they were not the only thing to watch for underfoot. Many of the streets in the centre, especially around the Münsterplatz, were rimmed by open streams or mini-canals, filled with streaming water. We believed they used to be a source of water for the town many centuries before, but in 1984, the Bächle, as they are known, were quite a pedestrian or cycling hazard for those unaware of their presence. And, like most places in Europe, when you dig, if you'll pardon the pun, the history was interesting. In this case the town's name was derived from its early incarnation as a silver mining community and the extensive mining rights that then belonged to the 'free miner'. It was a very pretty town; its Münster having escaped the terrible bombing that had obliterated towns of a similar vintage during the Second World War. There had been damage to older buildings though, many of which had been reconstructed, giving the town a faintly 'Disney-like' quality, with perfectly copied buildings standing where the original structures had been flattened.

Looking around and feeling hungry, we found a stall in the main market selling nothing but *apfelstrudel* and so I bought a very large portion for only Dm1.20 and it was melt-in-the-mouth perfect. But let's face it, if you're a fan of that particular treat, it's hard to find a bad one in Germany. While we were in the food mindset, we were drawn to a stall selling all the ingredients necessary to construct your own muesli, which we enthusiastically bought. We were slightly tempted by the unusually restrained brown arches of a McDonald's store, under the shade of a very old building, but we did resist … on that day.

'That must have been part of the conditions for occupying?' Jenny suggested.

And I was pretty sure she was right, as it was the first time that we had seen the famous 'golden arches' in such muted colours. But they did fit in with the rest of the decor on the surrounding buildings and didn't seem to be deterring the swarms of American tourists, who clearly hadn't travelled overseas to experience an immersion in country-specific European cuisine.

While we were in town, we explored the cost to send our leather jackets and possibly some of our other possessions back to the UK, so we would be a bit lighter on our travels. However, when we reached the train station, they were clearly used to shipping larger parcels than we had in mind. Ours was only going to be about five kilograms, and the scales didn't record such small weights. Also, the weighing machine was one of the older types that spat out a ticket after you stood on the scales – I hadn't seen that sort of machine since visiting Brighton Pier in the early 1970s. We scratched our heads and then Jenny had a very practical suggestion.

'Let's wear our leather jackets, then stand on the scales to see how much we weigh. Then we can take them off and weigh ourselves again, to work out the difference.'

Not terribly sophisticated, but typical lateral thinking by Jenny, when we were clearly dealing with a mid-twentieth century set of scales. Having completed this confusing exercise, and assuming the scales were accurate, we determined that our jackets would be less than five kilograms, so we could fit other items in to the parcel, to further lighten our cycling load. Having solved that particular puzzle, we headed to the nearest supermarket to load up on our essential supplies, and came away with food and a frisbee, which we tested when we got back to the camp site, to make certain that it wasn't faulty. It was a bit of fun, although on

Jenny's third throw the frisbee inexplicably found its way over a barbed wire fence, which gave me the opportunity of exploring the beautiful local countryside, during the 2 kilometre walk there and back to retrieve it.

Once we had decided to post our parcel, we needed to conform to European bureaucratic policies, by filling out Customs forms in both German and French. Then, strapping the parcel to my bike for the ride to the post office, we headed into town with our precious cargo. It was amazing what could be squeezed into the five-kilogram weight limit, and we lightened our load to the tune of two leather jackets, a frying pan, posters, one beach towel and two pairs of shoes – including the famous red high-heeled version, for which I and the Italian men of Sestri Levante had shown considerable appreciation. Then it was back via our now favourite muesli stall and it was time to lie in the sun at the camp site, giving our respective tans a bit of a top-up.

The next day, even though we had only been in Germany for two days, we were headed to France, in the form of Strasbourg. It wasn't any reflection on Germany or the Germans, but there was always the chance we would crisscross the Rhine, thereby moving between the two countries. To be fair, there was a history of the Germans and French regularly going back and forth, which you could see in the names either side of the Rhine River. Although in the nineteenth and twentieth centuries, those incursions had often been accompanied by rather more serious consequences for the German and French locals than merely name changes for the towns – during the Napoleonic for the Germans and then the Second World War, for the French.

In fact, after we had passed through the border and Jenny had a German stamp in her Australian passport, we were confronted by plenty of signs proclaiming the road on which we were travelling to be a part of the legendary Maginot Line. We couldn't see much more than a few overgrown pillboxes, but when it was built by the French in the 1930s, it was believed to be a state-of-the-art defence system to deter a German invasion, in case of another war. It had certainly been impressively substantial, impregnable from the air and unable to be levelled, possessing its own underground railway, and with advanced troop garrisons. However, when the Germans did invade France, they had been able to circumvent it from the north, through the low countries, making it irrelevant. Ever since then, the Maginot Line had become almost a dictionary definition for something that was very expensive to build but offered a false sense of security.

Despite this history, on a classic summer's day in 1984, with a clear blue sky and following a quiet road along the edge of the Rhine on our bikes, it was a very relaxing and peaceful ride. We stopped around lunchtime for our picnic in this peaceful, tree-lined setting, in the shade of a small football pavilion, and spread ourselves and our lunch out on the lush green grass. The only noise apart from our chatter was the buzz of the insects as they moved from flower to flower, and it would have been very easy to lie back and have a snooze. In fact, I did have to gently nudge Jenny when it was time for us to climb back on our bikes and resume our leisurely cycle – she insisted that she was just resting her eyes.

We saw quite a number of other cycle tourists that day, who were heading back towards our recent Rhine crossing location. We also passed a gaggle of older Germans who were clearly out for a slow cycle – one of our few overtaking opportunities on the entire trip to that point, apart from that downhill leg on one of Italy's mountainous roads. As we approached the town of Illkirch-Graffenstaden, the AA was rapidly losing more credibility for their directions and I had to ask a Frenchman, who was able to direct us. After 95 kilometres, even though it was on the flat, we were certainly grateful to find the camp site that the AA informed us was, 'Beside an artificial lake,' and that, 'There is a public bathing area, but quiet after 9 pm.'

'Good,' I said to Jenny. 'And hopefully no more noisy Germans belting out Queen at 3 am either!'

Although you could never be too careful. After all, we were close to the German border and the AA book had mentioned bathing. So, a bit like Arthur Dent in *The Hitchhiker's Guide to the Galaxy*, I was ever ready with my towel. When we did arrive, I had to conduct a long conversation in French, which turned out to be much easier than I expected after being out of that country for over a month. However, we discovered that no shops were open, so it was rice and sardines and an early-ish night after the long ride that day in the heat.

Following our meagre rations of the night before, we treated ourselves to an ultra-decadent breakfast of a one kilo block of chocolate and a litre of milk, from the local supermarket – convincing ourselves that we would probably burn those calories off by the middle of the day, if not sooner, given the heat and the distances we were covering every day. And we would need the energy, because we passed a sign later on the way into Strasbourg telling us that it was 36 degrees centigrade, which was even hotter than our ride into Florence, although a much shorter distance into this town, thankfully. When we made it to the centre, we found the impressive Strasbourg Cathedral, which easily dominated everything around it. It had a classically Gothic style, with a massive spire that seemed to disappear into the sky. The spire was completed in the fifteenth century, although there were a couple of the original eleventh century elements still intact that we could see, such as the crypt.

We were back in France again, so we thought we had better source some French bread and pâté for our lunch. Chaining our bikes to the railings close to the cathedral, we ambled off in the direction of the local *boulangerie*, where we were able to satisfy our cravings and then enjoy our bounty overlooking the Rhine. We also wanted to see the European Parliament, so we started walking along the river, following the signs. But after a few kilometres we realised it might be further than we had thought, so back to our bikes and a relatively long cycle to the parliament buildings. On such a hot day we were relieved when we made it inside the large modern building, especially as they had the air conditioning cranked up – not something we had experienced during our bike-and-tent regimen. As a British European, I was pleased to see that our taxes were being put to good use.

There was quite an impressive exhibition of Orwell's literary masterpiece, *Nineteen Eighty-Four*, and a large pictorial explanation of the European Council's work. Unsurprisingly though, they didn't have any photos of butter mountains, wine lakes, or sugar surpluses. I did also have the classic episode from the TV series *Yes Minister* bouncing around in my head, where Sir Humphrey advises the prime minister that those areas of European surplus are, 'the penalty we have to pay for trying to pretend we are Europeans'.

Of course, it was true that there were many British who were committed to the European ideal, but there was also a healthy scepticism, which cleverly satirical shows such as *Yes Minister* exploited to devastatingly funny effect.

When we emerged from the seat of European power, we were again hit by the intense heat of the day, so we hightailed it back to the camp and a refreshing swim in the bathing lake beside our tent. We also met a German chap who advised us that, despite the German side being interesting, we should stay on the French side if we wanted easier riding, until we reached a place called Wissembourg, when we should cross back into Germany. We had always planned to work out our route along the Rhine once we arrived there so, in the absence of any other information, he was our 'Tripadvisor' of 1984 – but with a much better command of English. Despite the heat, we cooked up a hearty German stew for dinner and, no surprise here, finished with a bar of chocolate. Thank heavens we were riding almost every day, or with all the chocolate we were eating, we would have started to resemble the Michelin man and woman. Fortunately, given our exercise over the previous two-and-a-half months, we were in fact steadily losing weight and gaining muscle mass – despite our clear dairy addiction.

The heat seemed to be building every day, so we decided the lazy option of lying in the sun and swimming in the lake would suit us very nicely the next day.

'We are on holiday, after all!' Jenny reminded me.

Easy to forget, when the daily routine of cycling to reach our next location took priority. Although, on that day, even Jenny with her perennial Aussie tan, was starting to feel it was too humid, while I was melting like an Italian gelato in the sun. So other than my five or six visits to the lake for a cool-off, we retired to the relative shade of the trees and our tent. The next day was the same for us, and when the alarm went off at

6:30 am, we looked at each other and decided that discretion was the better part of valour. Clearly the humidity and the riding were taking their toll. We also heard thunder and saw lightning in the distance, which didn't seem like a great environment in which to cycle to our next destination. Once the rain did hit it came with a pretty powerful wind, bending the trees around our tent perilously. So, after we had done our good deed for the day and saved our German neighbours' washing from the downpour, we retired to our tent, battened down the hatches for the night and hit the hay – hoping to wake with more energy the following day.

When we woke early in the morning, we felt pretty good, but just to be safe we bolstered our energy with a healthy serving of dairy. We gathered our possessions and bikes and headed off, via a tourist bureau, to our next destination, Seltz, 60 kilometres north of Strasbourg. Where we could, we would choose smaller roads, as we had done throughout our travels, to limit our exposure to the traffic and more importantly, the speed of the passing cars and trucks. This road was taking us through delightfully picturesque villages and towns, one of which had an archetypal *boulangerie*, selling warm and delicious bread, which we paired with local pâté and consumed by the side of the road for lunch. I was also continuing my slightly confusing interaction with the Rhine locals, being stopped by a German lady who spoke to me for a full thirty seconds in German, before she realised I had no idea what she was saying – my ginger hair and big frame looking every inch the northern German stereotype, as she explained to Jenny.

The ride was flat and very easy along the broad Rhine River Valley, which certainly wasn't exhibiting the type of mountainous diversions that the Italian engineers had found necessary to build into their roads. We were grateful for that consideration and the reliability of the terrain. And, while this was on the French side of the valley, and with apologies to the French, everything had a reliable Germanic feel to it. And the Germans were well known for their reliability on multiple dimensions – you always knew their trains and buses would arrive on time; their restaurants, shops and tourist venues would open when they said they would; and their cars would always work. Unfortunately, the latter was not something you could say for our recent Italian hosts, beautiful though their cars nearly always were. In fact, if you wanted to find a metaphor which most aptly demonstrated the difference between the Italians and the Germans, their performance cars would be near perfect, in my humble opinion.

We would experience that many years after our time in Europe when, living in Hong Kong, I had a hankering for a classic Italian marque. The car in question was ten years old, and I knew it wouldn't be perfect, but the Maserati I was set on buying had a low growl like a hunting lion. It also looked beautiful, in a very sleek Italian way and you felt it probably should come with its very own pair of wraparound sunglasses. My antennae should have been up earlier, when I walked into a Maserati showroom which sold new cars, to get a feel for what they *should* be like, even though my intended version would be considerably older. The showroom manager asked what I had driven before, found out they had been German cars, and went on to inform me that: 'With an Italian car, you need to look past the occasional reliability issues and focus on the beauty, the intense nature of the sound and the performance on the road.'

He was right, because all those things put a smile on my face, every time I slipped into the beautifully upholstered leather seats and started the engine with its signature sound. However, it would have been appreciated even more if the car had spent as much time on the road 'performing' as it did in the repair shop. The German cars, in contrast, mostly looked functional and had some nice touches, but didn't turn people's heads as they cruised by – however, you could rely on them always being *available* to cruise by, because they were mostly bulletproof from an engineering perspective. Even in 1984, the German-made Volkswagen Kombi was known to be virtually indestructible, which was why so many antipodeans used them to tour Europe.

In the Rhine River Valley, well before we could contemplate owning even a Kombi, we were enjoying the comparatively easy riding and reliability of the German-engineered roads and found our camp site with little trouble. Later that evening, as we polished off another serving of Jenny's signature sardine risotto, I was wondering whether a car of some sort might have been a good idea after all – my left knee had developed some worrying pains when cycling hard. Even though I had raised the seat to try to stretch it out some more, I didn't want to injure myself in the final stages, and before the start of the new rugby season. These days, we would have instantly sought some advice from a sports physiotherapist, of which there would be plenty in almost every town. However, in 1984, neither of us had ever thought about using a physio and they certainly weren't as ubiquitous as they are now. That has certainly changed and, as I have aged, but kept playing sport, I'm sure that I have educated at least one of my physio's children through private school and probably paid for a few overseas family holidays in addition. Whenever I call him to book in for treatment for a new injury, I can imagine him ringing off and opening BMW's home page, to browse for the latest models, in anticipation of my long and relatively expensive recovery process.

The next morning on the Rhine, we had every intention of an early start, but the dew was heavy and our tent too wet to pack, so we gratefully went back to the land of nod. We did need to get to the Rhine crossing by 9:30 am though, so we finally packed up and made it just in time. We were heading for Walldorf on the German side, but we didn't get very far before we spotted a shop selling classical German brown rye bread and Teewurst – a traditional German spread, which seemed to consist of finely ground pork and beef, with a smoky taste. Assuming Jenny's translation was accurate, of course. Having polished off quite a lot of those two very filling staples, we climbed back onto our bikes and started to see multiple cycling tracks leading off beside the road. They often seemed to head into towns or meander into forests and they weren't signposted, so we figured they were for the locals and stayed on our main road.

On this leg, we had been using a Michelin map, but it ended 10 kilometres south of Walldorf.

'Let's just stay on this road and we should get there,' Jenny suggested.

That made sense to me, until we hit the roadblock and detour signs. We then had a quick route-planning discussion and agreed we should put our large Collins road atlas to use. It was less detailed, but at least it went all the way to Walldorf. As we were debating our route, Jenny belatedly spotted a sign for a cycle path, which suggested it too would finish in Walldorf, so we packed our map book away and cycled off with high hopes. The path did lead all the way to the town, although it went there via a forest track, with exposed tree roots, ruts, fallen branches and scores of pine cones scattered around the pathway. Not ideal on heavily laden touring bikes, but this appeared to be our only obvious route, so we persevered. Along the way we met a few older riders who kept us on the right path, and we eventually rejoined a road with signs to Walldorf. At that point, we needed to find our camp site, so we consulted the AA, which informed us that: 'The site lies near a swimming pool in the woods.' That was the extent of their directions. We should be able to find that if we stayed on this pathway, we thought; although we did need to stop and talk to a local girl, who eventually directed Jenny to our home for the night.

We arrived quite sore, with various aches and pains starting to compound after almost three months on our bikes, so we weren't really in the mood to be told that we would have to pay extra to bring our bikes into the camping grounds. Really? This was the first time we had been asked to pay for them in all the time we had been on the Continent, and it did seem to be rather mean-spirited. It wasn't as if they were going to take up any extra space and we clearly weren't the wealthiest campers they were going to see that summer. Still, not much we could do about it, so we paid up, told them what we thought of their policy and then each spent at least half an hour in the hot showers, for which we weren't paying any extra.

'That'll show them!' we said in unison.

We had ridden 85 kilometres that day and, while it hadn't been the sort of mountainous terrain that we had experienced on the Italian Riviera, our bodies, and our minds, were starting to tire. We'd see how we felt in the morning, but I had the distinct sense that it wouldn't take very much to convince us to accelerate our transition up to the Netherlands, via an alternate transport, like the train.

The next day, we had a leisurely stroll into Heidelberg, from our camp site in Walldorf, for necessities and luxuries – pastries and choccies, obviously. We were self-medicating for our various injuries, on the basis that we needed energy, and we hoped sugar and dairy-based treats would give us that boost. Seemed like a theory we could get behind. There were now several factors we had to consider on our trip and which we discussed at length. The first of those was that my knee injury seemed to be worsening, although with regular stretching and daily massages from Jenny, I would be prepared to push through it. The second was an Aussie friend of Jenny's who was getting married in London in late July, and whose wedding she was keen to attend if possible. The third, and possibly the most compelling, was that the weather forecast for the rest of the summer in Northern Europe was very wet. That pattern had already started to make the earlier part of this trip less comfortable than we had hoped and, as I now reminded Jenny in turn: 'This trip was always meant to be a holiday!'

If this had been the start of the trip, maybe we would have persevered. But after nearly three months on our bikes, we didn't fancy the idea of repeating the moist experiences we'd had in the French and Italian Rivieras. Also, after giving it at least five seconds thought, Jenny had inexplicably declined to administer the self-diagnosed, daily massage routine for my knee and surrounding areas, even though I generously offered to buy the massage oil! So, everything considered, we decided we would cut out some of the Rhine cycling and lower parts of the Netherlands and aim to spend more time in Amsterdam.

Looking at the positives, we would have more money left when we arrived back in the UK, which would no doubt come in handy. There would also be plentiful supplies of massage oil for my injury in Amsterdam, so it wouldn't be too late for Jenny to come to my aid, in case she changed her mind!

As if to reinforce our decision, the rain was coming down in torrents early the next day, so there was no way we could pack or ride, even if it did stop, everything being so wet. When it eventually stopped, we caught a bus into Heidelberg, to check out our train options for the next day and have a walking tour of this interesting old town. It sits in the shadow of the ruins of Heidelberger Schloss – initially a fifteenth century castle, then a sixteenth century palace for the ruling dynasty. That day, however, we were drawn to Macca's which of course was crawling with American tourists, and we finally succumbed to the lure of that ubiquitous fast food.

When we walked inside, Jenny turned to me and said: 'I think you're going to like this place.'

'Why's that,' I said, nervously eyeing the large number of jostling American tourists in front of us.

'Because, if you glance at the menus above the counter, you'll notice they're serving beers with their burgers!'

'Outstanding,' I said. 'They'd sell a lot more McDonald's meals in London and Sydney if they adopted that approach there.'

Clearly the Germans had convinced the American parent company that beer was a staple 'food'. Good for them, we thought. So, unexpectedly refreshed by our alcoholic Big Mac meal, and with plenty of wet weather to keep us inside, battle was recommenced in our European Scrabble championship, although modesty prohibits me from declaring that round's winner – still, I did have an awful lot of ground to make up.

'Fantastic – a dry tent!' I called to Jenny the next day after venturing outside.

Unfortunately, I spoke too soon, and it started raining again. Oh, well, there was nothing for it but to pack it up wet, or we would never be leaving at that rate. So, all packed up, we rode off into the 'rain-set'. While it wasn't as bad as our experience on the way to Spotorno, the rain in the Rhine Valley was persistent. We had decided to make a quick detour into the Amex office and were grateful we did, as my mum had wired me some more money from my account, which would mean we were quite 'flush' again.

'Amsterdam, here we come,' I laughingly said to Jenny.

Before buying the tickets, we had intended to go to Arnhem and then cycle northwards from there. However, we were a little worried still by the rain forecasts, the prospect of seeing less of Amsterdam and missing the wedding deadline at the end of the month, if we became stranded in Arnhem. So, we decided to head straight for Amsterdam. As the train took us northwards through the Rhine Valley, we passed scores of picturesque castles, hamlets, and vineyards, in a valley that was heavily serviced by cycle paths, especially from Bingen onwards. We were a little disappointed to miss the experience of that part of the journey, as it seemed it would have been one of the easier legs, but on balance, we were keen to see Amsterdam, so that would have to wait for another trip.

CHAPTER 10
Amsterdam and home

Arriving in a large city like Amsterdam late in the day, there was no point trying to find a camp site, nor did we yet have our bikes, which had been consigned separately. So, we booked into a hotel called The Smash, stored half our baggage in lockers at the station and caught another train to what turned out to be a very-easy-to-find and clean hotel – great name too. Having just arrived, we weren't yet sure what Dutch food looked like, but we had plenty of hard-won expertise in Italian food. We found a traditional-looking Italian restaurant just around the corner from our hotel and very close to the infamous red-light district. The restaurant was good and certainly affordable – pizza, beer, wine, and a ten percent tip only cost us the equivalent of three pounds each.

The next day we were revelling in our 'luxury', with an actual bed, hot showers on tap and a large Dutch breakfast – bread, cheese, sliced meats, pastries, chocolate spread, *stroop* (a thick, dark-brown sugar syrup, pronounced similar to 'rope'), apple, peanut butter, and tea. Quite an eclectic mix, but if this much dairy and meat was a part of their diet every day, I was already starting to understand why the Dutch were, on average, so tall.

Refreshed and ready to take on the day, we headed to the train station on the off-chance that our bikes would be ready; and they were. Fantastic, we thought, promptly hopped on them, and started following our noses to the camp site, which was just outside the centre of the city.

I had forgotten our main learnings from the previous large towns that we had visited – it could often become confusing, with multiple routes signposted out of town, making it tricky for cyclists to work out which direction was best. Although, in Amsterdam, we should also have realised that the routes close to town were virtually built around cyclists and their needs. This became much clearer when we cycled back to the information centre, having become lost. The helpful lady in the centre furnished us with directions: follow the cycle path to the free ferry over the river, close to the train station, and then follow the abundant signs along more cycle paths to our camp site.

'I'm glad we asked, or we would have been riding in the wrong direction for ages,' Jenny pointed out. She was good like that, alerting me to instances when I may have acted in haste, without all the necessary information.

When we did find the camp site, it was cheap, basic but clean. It was also populated with a variety of characters, many of whom appeared to have come directly from Woodstock or some other drug-fuelled 1960s concert, and never gone home. It was interesting to say the least!

We were looking forward to exploring the city and doing so on our bikes, having realised that Amsterdam catered for this form of transport better than any other city on the planet, at that time. Our first experience didn't let us down either. We found cycle lanes on pretty well every street, including smaller back roads. Each of those cycle lanes was safely separated from the traffic and had its own traffic lights, with small, dedicated bicycle symbols. After about half an hour on our bikes we started to understand why though – there were more cyclists than there were cars and it was clear that, in a complete reversal from Italy and France, the cyclists had the dominant right of way in nearly every circumstance.

'This is brilliant,' I called out to Jen.

'Yep, I'm feeling much safer on these lanes,' she replied.

Jenny was obviously enjoying the sensation of safety on the road, without a need to be on high alert for rogue drivers. We hadn't always felt entirely safe on the roads until that point, and it meant we could relax and take in the scenery more easily than we had in large towns in France or Italy. Although we did quickly discover that, while cars gave cyclists much more room, that was not always true of our fellow cyclists. They weren't afraid to use their bells and let you know if you were holding them up on what must have been a regular commute for many of them.

So, we kept cycling through the back streets and beside the ubiquitous canals, until we stumbled across a section of the red-light district that was strangely familiar to me.

'I recognise this street,' I called out to Jenny.

I should have realised that might not garner the sort of reaction I had been hoping for, given the street was chock full of brothels and questionable establishments. I had to hastily explain that this was the street where our hotel had been when I toured as a young man with my rugby club in 1980 on the annual Easter tour. I'm not sure that explanation would have helped either, on reflection. Anyway, my best mate, Nigel, and I had been 'sponsored' on that tour by a few of the older club tourists and we quickly found out why when we arrived – they needed some younger guys who would stay *relatively* sober, and also not partake of the abundant 'joints' available in most bars. Also, to keep tabs on them when they were out and about in the clubs at night, so someone would be available to get them back to the hotel in one piece.

It seemed that availability also extended to the rugby pitches during the games. After all, this was well before professional rugby and the Dutch teams, while being accommodating, weren't of a very high standard. This meant that rugby wasn't the main attraction for all the English clubs, who descended annually on Amsterdam at that time of year. As a result, the games were a little more 'relaxed'. Our youthful 'responsibilities' during those games extended to ensuring that the more mature members of the team wouldn't be forced to undertake too much exertion. We were also tasked, where possible, to try to guide the play back to the place where, on more than one occasion, our more 'mature' front row had failed to rise from the previous scrum, due to being a little 'tired and emotional' from the previous evening's activities.

However, as they say, 'what goes on tour stays on tour,' so the specifics will have to remain shrouded in a touring cloak of anonymity. All I will say is that, on that tour at least, I watched with fascination the staying power and dedication of some of the more experienced tourists. They clearly took their responsibilities as visitors of that great city seriously and were intent on heavily investing both time and money into the Amsterdam community over that four-day tour. In 1984, Jenny and I were taking Amsterdam in a much more restrained manner and at a more sedate pace. After we had walked our bikes along some interesting streets, where window-shopping had a whole different connotation, we thought we had better ride back to our camping ground. This involved an experience that was unique, for us at least. As we waited for the ferry at around 5 pm, we were in what I can only describe as a rush hour 'bicycle jam', with upwards of two hundred bikes waiting to crowd onto the ferry, to go home from work or university. It was strange, but we were starting to miss the novelty of being two of the very few cyclists on the road further south in Europe.

When we rode back in again the next day, it was almost possible to feel like a local on our mode of transport. It was interesting that, despite the bike-obsessed nature of many French and Italians when it came to the sport, there was no way we would have been happy cycling into the centre of Rome, Florence, Marseille or Paris in the 1980s. Obviously, we would have been quite safe from cars cycling into Venice, although the locals would have objected, I suspect, as they dived off the narrow paths into the canals to get out of our way. Having said there weren't many queues of cars in Amsterdam, we did then see one unusual procession of vehicles, as we sat by one of the picturesque canals devouring the pastries we had just bought. It was a parade of two hundred-plus vintage cars, circa 1940s, which were evidently making the well-known Paris–Moscow–Paris journey and looked like they were being escorted by most of the police force in Amsterdam.

We had a few days left before we had to leave for the UK, but we wanted to be well organised in advance, so we bought tickets for our homeward leg to London. Our journey would take us via the Hook of Holland, Harwich and finally into Liverpool Street station. We also managed to connect with Jenny's family, to assure them that we were alive and prospering, using the Dutch phone cables, which must have been made from a different material to those troublesome Italian varieties, because they worked properly. We hadn't yet consigned our bikes at the train station, as they were still an important transport source, especially in Amsterdam, so we weren't letting them go until the last minute. Having said that, we didn't need them the next day as we caught a bus and walked to Anne Frank House. It was a well curated exhibition that touched on the anti-Semitism which had sprung up since the war in many parts of Eastern Europe. I found it very direct and confronting. The museum was a quiet place to sit and to reflect on what must have been a terrifying time for the Jewish population of Europe.

We were also clearly starting to slip back into our London personas, because that day we were tempted into a Burger King for another non-local experience. It was pleasant having someone else prepare a meal for us and the fries were a treat we hadn't experienced for some months. We weren't quite sure what to make of the local food scene and, as far as we could tell, there didn't appear to be the same central theme and emphasis on local food in Amsterdam as there had been in France and Italy. Following our slip back into fast-food territory, Jen suggested we walk it off and take a look around the world-famous red-light district. So, we wandered over to look at the infamous 'girls-in-the-windows' street and, on the way, we were constantly approached by strangers brazenly asking whether we wanted to buy hash or cocaine. We also saw several of what they called 'headshops' where they sold equipment of nearly every conceivable variety to smoke dope. Not our thing, but interesting nonetheless.

'I guess when someone in Amsterdam offers you mushrooms for dinner, you need to be careful,' I said to Jenny.

'What do you mean?' she asked.

'Well, based on what we've seen, you'd want to be sure that it was in a sauce or side dish accompanying your meal, and not in a cake or tea, at the end of the meal!'

Having come through our brush with the seamier side of Amsterdam unscathed, we decided some fresh air via one more road trip on our bikes would be exactly what the doctor ordered. We took a 20-kilometre cycle north of Amsterdam to a town called Markham. With the flat road, this was a breeze for us, and it only took 45 minutes to get there, even though the flat landscape enabled a strong wind to blow into our faces all the way. It was a small and picturesque town and we even saw wooden clogs sitting outside the doors of a few older houses along the way – though I did wonder if they had been placed there more for the tourists than as a genuine item of household footwear. Because we were newly affluent and ending our trip a little sooner than we had originally planned, we splashed out on a decent lunch. I then sprinted around the town buying presents for everyone at home. Jenny had been more organised; her pressies were a combination of the countries through which we had passed, whereas my family would be getting a decidedly Dutch version of our trip. Still, I hadn't wanted to carry extra gear all around

Europe, and any extra weight had seemed to make it onto my panniers as we went.

We briefly called my home to let them know we would be back early and then we went out into the town for our 'big last meal'. Given the Netherland's colonial and strong seafaring history, it was no surprise that you could find pretty well any cuisine you wanted in Amsterdam. We chose Indonesian and we found what seemed to be a reasonably upmarket restaurant, if such a thing was possible, where we consumed a massive 'rice table for two'. This was our first experience of this cuisine and it seemed to be a very agreeable combination of Indian and Chinese dishes. We also had some pre-dinner drinks (or PDDs) in a small bar, followed by a litre of Liebfraumilch – I couldn't believe we were back to that English-Sunday-lunch staple. Not bad for Florin 40 each and a ten percent tip. To end the night, we strolled to the station, having to again pass through the red-light district and back to our tent, feeling very content.

We were nearing the end of our time in Amsterdam and on the Continent, but there were a few more things we were hoping to do before we left. We had a light breakfast, Dutch style, but Jenny had a hankering for more dairy. So, into McDonald's we went – we had passed a few other American fast-food chains to get to this one, because according to my cycling companion: 'The thick shakes are better at Macca's.'

That might have been true, but we had to again contend with a posse of loud American tourists. I was thinking back to my strong aversion to people talking loudly in small public places. I had wondered if that was only me as an Englishman, but apparently not, because the locals who had ventured into the restaurant were clearly not impressed either.

Following our brush with the stereotypical American-tourists-in-Europe, we headed for something much more local – the Amsterdam Diamond Centre. Jen was keen to experience it and Amsterdam was, after all, famous for diamonds, having been a trading centre since the sixteenth century when diamond cutting had been established there. She was very happy to ogle, and we watched some skilled polishing of a diamond – we also learned that most diamonds have an average of fifty-eight 'facets' and they are all supposed to be symmetrical. I wasn't quite sure why Jenny was so interested, but I had a niggling feeling that this new information might end up costing me some money at some point in the future. We then made a beeline for the Van Gogh Museum, but it seemed to be pretty expensive and only focused on one artist, obviously. So, we headed to the Rijksmuseum and, while it too was expensive, there were multiple artists there, a larger variety of exhibits and some very fine examples of Dutch masters. We both loved Rembrandt's *The Night Watch*. Jenny was busy converting me from a philistine.

I had been vaguely aware that the British and the Dutch had their own share of history, but it was brought home to me literally when we came across an exhibit in that museum, of the oldest captured Union Jack in existence. I recalled from history lessons, an infamous raid by the Dutch Navy on the British in Chatham during the seventeenth century. If you were Dutch, I imagine it *was* famous, because a large British flagship had been captured and towed back to the Netherlands, during one of four British–Dutch naval conflicts. Of course, with both the Dutch and the British East India companies competing for colonial footholds and trading rights, this conflict was bound to happen. It continued in periodic bursts across two centuries, until the rise of the British and the French empires reduced the Netherlands and their navy to a shadow of its former greatness. Interestingly though, despite this largely forgotten enmity between the two great trading nations, there was little-to-no lingering resentment in the way the French and the English had managed to cultivate that rivalry on an ongoing basis.

Having finished our cultural tour of Amsterdam at the museum we made it back to our camp site and relaxed catching up on the news in the UK, with a long, leisurely read of the *Sunday Times* and supplement. We had one more full day to enjoy the delights of Amsterdam, but first we had to consign our 'best friends' and constant companions to the Dutch train service. We'd learnt our lessons from other towns and stored the remaining panniers ready for our trip the next day – apart from the tent, obviously. We then treated ourselves to another Macca's thick shake, but without the annoyingly loud tourists this time, and started to wander around the town.

We'd been to the Rijksmuseum and Anne Frank House, and we had decided not to visit the Rembrandt Museum, but we did want to spend time simply strolling around the older parts of the city. A bit like Paris, it was fun to wander around without a fixed agenda, with canal-centred streets at almost every turn, crammed with quaint multicoloured houses. We were surprised to learn that it had some similarities with Venice, with many of the older and well-preserved houses built on very large piles, which had been driven through an upper layer of mud into the firm, sandy bottom below. There were many thousands of buildings that stretched as far back as the sixteenth century. Some of the bridges we saw were also still the original wooden construction, including the Magere Brug (Skinny bridge in English), one of the oldest. With all of this wandering, we needed some fuel and, though we weren't quite eating like locals with our hot chocolate and donut snack, we were aiming to re-acclimatise before we entered the normality of our London existence. Dinner was a challenge because we had left our camping stove at the train station locker, so a final dinner it was of crisps and sweets before bed – plenty of calories and dairy through the day, but we'd need to up our veggie intake on our return anyway.

Our final day on the Continent after three-and-a-half months had dawned and we were both sad and excited.

Jen summed it up quite well when she told me, 'I'm looking forward to sleeping in a bed every night.'

'Fair enough. I'm looking forward to not having to pack our tent every morning,' I replied.

Clearly, we were both just about ready to move back into our lives in London. We had set the alarm early – well, *I* had set it early because I don't like being late. No surprise that I had struggled with the Italian sense of time then. Jenny was much more 'just-in-time' with her timekeeping and was seemingly more relaxed about being late. Something that has been a theme between us over the decades – they do say that 'opposites attract'. On this occasion though, much to her disgust, we were up at 6:20 am. This meant we arrived at the station by 8 am, well in time for our departure. The trip was very smooth with a short train ride to Hook of Holland and then a six-hour ferry ride to Harwich, in Essex.

Europe was turning on the weather for our last day, so we migrated up onto the sundeck of the ferry for a while to capture some of the 'bennys'. Then, because we could, we watched a movie, from which one iconic line has since become a well-worn catchcry for doing something you *really* don't want to do: 'I'd rather stick needles in my eyes!'

I'll leave you to work out which movie I'm talking about, but it was very good. We were on our way home to the UK, but on this trip, there was no Brownies troop to make us tea and cake, so we plumped for a meal of roast chicken and chips, with lots of gravy – thank heavens in retrospect that the crossing was calm.

Once we reached Blighty, the train trip from Harwich to Liverpool Street was quite short and we were both pleased to be back in a place where English was the first language. We knew this to be true, but if you had been a tourist listening to the muffled and mostly incomprehensible platform announcements coming over the tannoy at Liverpool Street that day, you would have been forgiven for checking that it was, in fact, the case. We knew this station well though, and once we had navigated our way to the underground section, we were able to sit back and relax all the way to Rayners Lane, which was the closest on the 'Met' line to my parents' place. It was amazing to both of us how 'relaxed' we felt now we were in a place where we mostly understood what was going on. And, where we could easily navigate our way around, without reference to maps, but where if we did become disoriented, a simple enquiry to a fellow countryman would mostly put us back on track.

When we arrived at our final destination, without our previously consigned bikes, and being quite late, there was no sense in trying to find a bus and struggle with the panniers, so we splashed out on a local taxi, and were home one hour after we had arrived in Central London. Obviously, neither of us had taken a house key around Europe with us, my parents were themselves overseas, and of course my brother was out on the town. So, I had to scramble around in the dark looking for a spare key, which fortunately was where it was supposed to be in the rose garden. Home again, we gratefully dropped our gear in my room, found the remnants of the food and drink my brother had left in the fridge, and sank in front of the TV with a couple of self-satisfied sighs. We'd done it! Now we knew we were home, so we staggered off to a comfortable bed, in an actual house, and dreamt about cycling and Europe.

Epilogue

As we reflected on our adventure in the days that followed our return to England, and answered the many questions from friends and families about our journey, we found ourselves unpacking both our kit and our memories. There were so many special moments, but one constant and unexpected theme, to which we were uniquely exposed given our mode of transport, was the vagaries of the weather patterns and specifically the rainstorms that covered most of Europe in the spring and summer of 1984. The good news was that we had packed some basic rain gear and our tent had survived the constant deluge very well – although by Amsterdam, it was starting to show signs that it would not continue for much longer. We knew how it felt!

Having said that, it was only water and, while rain seemed to be either an occurrence or a threat much of the time, it didn't dampen our spirits, if you'll pardon the pun – even when we were trapped under a road tunnel outside of Spotorno in Italy, with passing motorists spraying us, as a bonus. After all, we had the privilege of travelling at our leisure through some of the most beautiful scenery in Europe and enjoying experiences that most tourists will never have. The benefit of cycle touring, I think. Also, when we lived day to day on our own wits, in situations and languages where we were not always sure what was and wasn't acceptable, we gained a new appreciation for what we had in our regular, daily lives. We built a resilience and self-confidence that can't easily be achieved under normal circumstances. As a result of this and my earlier round-the-world trip, via a year in Australia, I was convinced that travelling under your own steam was something every young person should be encouraged to attempt – if they were fortunate enough to be able to do so. Later in life, I've found both as an employer and a parent, that independent travel can mature young people immeasurably and give them confidence in their decision-making abilities. It can be worth many years of work experience, in the way it shapes personalities.

In our own lives, when both our children reached the end of their school years and before university, we certainly encouraged them to travel and they have benefitted from that experience, possibly more so because they funded it themselves. It has also brought out their own adventurer genes and both have travelled to an amazingly diverse selection of countries, demonstrating a sense of enterprise and enquiring minds. Our son, Nick, often on his own and with nothing but a pack and language skills, has done everything from riding a motorbike from Santiago to Patagonia, while on university exchange in Chile, to travelling around Australia and South-East Asia, working on prawn trawlers. He's also bedded down in remote villages on the Vietnam–China border. And our daughter, Katy, toured Europe and then later took her own, more expansive cycle-touring trip – cycling from Birchgrove in Sydney to Budapest, crossing large tracts of Australia, South-East Asia and both Western and Eastern Europe along the way. A remarkable trip that tested someone who had previously been a nervous traveller. She and her boyfriend cycled their way through fifteen countries, covering almost 8,000 kilometres, over 257 days. Our trip appears positively tame compared to some of their adventures, but we hope we might have encouraged them to take the leap.

Reflecting on our trip in 1984, we had made a few pre-journey purchases that we hoped would make the whole experience a little smoother – the AA camping book, the Collins road atlas, the Readers Digest cycle maintenance book and a *Travel Scrabble* set. Despite my comments along the way, the AA book proved invaluable most of the time, and we forgave them when they had clearly skipped some parts of Europe where we were seeking to lay our weary heads. Our map book allowed us to plan, although we would have preferred something more compact on the journey. We couldn't quite bring ourselves to part with this route planner – which proved to be a wise decision when we found ourselves in parts of Europe where Michelin were not providing guidance.

It might have been helpful to know a little more about the topography of the valleys and mountains before we struck them, or our unintentional detours when we became directionally challenged. However, it was often when we had unplanned stops, or were forced into alternate paths due to weather, that we experienced the local environment and countries in a way I think we would otherwise have missed – such as the family in Guilherand who invited us into their home, or the many fellow cyclists with whom we interacted. Had we been looking down at a phone map, rather than looking up at the people and places we were passing, we would have mostly missed those interactions. Maybe that's why Jenny and I still like to find those increasingly rare physical maps when we can, to plan trips and even have with us for reference, as we navigate our way around. Because even though we are both technologically capable, we like to allow those random and chance interactions to occur and also to be in control of our own destinies, rather than be at the behest of an algorithm from a technology company, no matter how smart it may be.

Our cycle maintenance efforts were fortunately not tested as much as we had feared, though when we did need to make running adjustments, the Readers Digest manual gave me the confidence to attempt them, and that mostly helped us keep the bikes moving.

On a sidenote, we owed a debt of thanks to the chap in the original bike shop in Richmond who suggested we needed those thick, inner tube, puncture protectors. When we took them out on our return home, they were literally pitted with indentations, which would have been tens of punctures on each wheel, without those handy additions. Our final pre-ride purchase, excepting the bikes and tent, had been the Scrabble set and it was a masterstroke of a suggestion from Jenny before we left. It was amazing how much entertainment a very small and very portable game, and one that has been around for ever, could provide. It tested our brains and engaged our competitive instincts in a relatively benign manner. Thank you JW Spears!

I'll get to the bikes and tent, but if I consider our other most valuable asset on the trip, disregarding the wet weather gear for a moment, I'd have to say it was a tie between our Swiss Army knife and our phrasebook. The latter was particularly useful in Italy, as neither of us could speak the language. The Swiss Army knife was invaluable in many situations, allowing us to make running adjustments to bikes, open cans of food and beer, take corks from wine bottles, cut string to make running repairs, sew flags onto panniers, cut hair, see small print on the maps with the magnifying glass, and many other small but important tasks. We didn't need the implements that allowed us to de-scale a fish or take a stone out of a horse's hoof, but you could never be too prepared. I could understand why it had continued to be one of the Swiss nation's more successful and famous exports – apart from their discrete banking services, of course.

When we turned our minds to the least valuable belongings on the trip, I had been tempted to say it was our beach towels. They were certainly quite bulky, and if we had access to the sort of micro towels available these days, we would have had so much more space. Also, we weren't dependent on them in the same way Arthur Dent was as he hitchhiked his way around the Galaxy, or the average German tourist seemed to be. But, despite their size, we did need them for daily showering and the occasional swimming excursion in the Mediterranean, so they were essential. On balance, and despite the appreciation Jenny had received for them in Sestri Levante that one night, it would probably be those red high-heeled shoes, which I discovered part way around the trip, at the bottom of my panniers.

Moving to our tent and bikes, we were very happy with both purchases, and they literally got us around Europe in one piece. Our tent was our home for three-and-a-half months and served us better than we could ever have hoped, especially given the weather often forced us to stay inside for extended periods of time. It also played a positive role in extinguishing my traumatic Welsh hillside cub scout experience and associated reluctance to ever camp again. Although, by the time we had finished our European tour, I did feel that I had stored up enough camping experience to last me the rest of my life. After a few weeks, and when we had overcome our reluctance to ever set foot inside a tent again, we did set it up once in my parents' garden, to determine whether it was still likely to be serviceable. But when we had a thorough look at the seams and the inner tent, we knew that we wouldn't be using it again, even if we had retained any desire to camp … which we most definitely had not.

Our bikes turned out to be brilliant investments and, despite my whingeing about the hills and the occasional mishaps, they lasted remarkably well, required very little maintenance, and carried us and our possessions around Europe – through towns large and small; along river valleys; over hills and mountains, including the infamous Passo del Bracco in Italy; and even through forests. We were thrilled with them and grateful to the bike shop who sold them to us; and to Ernie Clements, one of the great British post-war racers, whose design had inspired them. And, as the Readers Digest suggested they would in their maintenance book, if well cared for, they lasted very well. Once we had cleaned and serviced them following their European adventure, we were able to sell them for close to the original purchase price – resulting in two new happy owners and two very happy sellers.

Along with our irreplaceable experiences en route, when we returned and started slotting back into our everyday life in London, we found our trip had other unexpected benefits. We noticed that we were a *lot* fitter than we had been before we left. Not surprising maybe, but one unexpected translation for me was that I was able to play tennis and rugby at a higher level of capability and intensity than I had ever done previously. Clearly, I hadn't had any opportunity to practice my rugby passing, sidestepping, or kicking skills while cycling around Europe, so I can't have been as fit as I thought I was before we left! Amazing what regular incidental exercise and a healthy, balanced diet with high dairy intake can achieve. Obviously, I should have been consuming more chocolate and dairy products previously, and I would do my best to remedy that oversight now we had returned.

Our language skills had been tested from the start. Highlighted initially in that camp site in Provence, where my inability to adequately discuss Sacha Distel's appearance in the pantheon of great French singers left both parties in confusion. And, during my regular interactions with those French phone operators, who seemed to be masquerading everywhere as truculent customer service representatives, and where the Gallic shrug or pout was completely pointless. Or, while trying to negotiate in Italian for a pack of cards that had the required number for our intended game, or our daily supply of pasta and pastries. Despite these obvious inadequacies on my part, my French language skills seemed to work surprisingly well – even in Italy! Jenny's German likewise worked well, once she overcame her initial shyness to speak, although we didn't really spend as much time in that country to properly test it out. In Italy, despite falling back on French regularly, by the time we left that country, we both had a working knowledge of the basics, and Jenny's arm-waving and gestures had truly reached an inspirational level of communication, which even some of the Italians couldn't help but admire.

And then there was the food and wine. We arrived home knowing a lot more about what good wine should taste like, and good food, for that matter, and we developed a lifelong and deep appreciation for Italian food. In France and Italy, we found ourselves routinely being educated by owners, waiters and sommeliers in restaurants, regarding the 'provenance' of their food and wine. We usually didn't need to ask; they took it to be part of their job to inform us. On our return, when we tried to engage in similar conversations in our local restaurants, we often provoked looks of confusion or just a WTF response in 1980s Britain. I recall one such conversation in one of our local Italian trattorias, which by the way, did produce very tasty food. The waiter had just brought the menu where we had spotted a bottle of Chianti from a particular Tuscan region that we wanted to try, having been there recently. It didn't show as much detail as we wanted on the menu, so I asked, 'Hi, can you tell us which year it is please?'

'*Si*, it's 1984.'

Smart-arse, I thought.

'Sorry, I meant which year is the wine?'

'Not sure, but the answer might still be 1984.'

'Okay, thanks .... don't bother decanting it!'

We certainly didn't want to become one of those wine or food snobs, who seemed to delight in making others feel inadequate about the things they didn't know – we've all listened to those people, loudly proclaiming their knowledge, or lecturing their table, and the restaurant. But we had now been alerted to the fact, often by the people who produced the wines, that certain wines and foods went together rather well. Also, that the wine vintage and certain characteristics were important, such as the region of production, in addition to the type of grapes used in the blends.

While in Europe we had also tried to embrace that Italian saying: *'Una cena senza vino è come un giorno senza sole'* – 'A meal without wine is like a day without sunshine.'

So, we were keen to continue learning and experimenting,

especially with wine. And with experience over the years, as I have been fortunate to travel the world in my work, I've come to realise the limits of one person's knowledge – there is so much to understand and now so many wine-producing countries, regions, vineyards, and grape varieties, that unless it's your business to know what goes with what, keeping abreast of it all is unlikely to be possible for the average punter. As a result, I've made it a habit to ask the owner, waiter, or sommelier for recommendations in most restaurants, and I have drunk some truly great wines, which we would never have tried otherwise.

There's a metaphor for life in there somewhere, I'm sure.

Of course it makes sense to do your research, if you're able to do so, and then make an informed decision. But I never cease to be amazed at the number of people who eschew the advice of experts in many fields, trying to conquer all the information themselves, to understand the area – when it would be much better to ask someone whose job it is to understand and dispense advice. After all, you wouldn't try to become an expert on medicines and treat yourself if you were sick – you'd consult a doctor. Okay, that's a bit more life and death than say choosing a bottle of wine to go with your spaghetti marinara, but the principle is the same. If someone is paid to become an expert in something, and you can satisfy yourself that they know what they are talking about, then it's worth asking their opinion to aid your own decision-making process.

And what of Europe? The European ideal has certainly been through many ups and downs since that time and, while unity clearly had, and still has many economic and political benefits, the will to retain the individuality and independence of nationality is unlikely to disappear – despite Brussels' best endeavours. After all, the Italians, the French, the Germans, the Swiss and the Dutch are very different in many ways and, despite our reflections and realisation of how closely 'related' Europeans may have been back in 1984, long may those differences remain.

Without wishing to sound like one of those *Monty Python* Yorkshiremen, explaining to all and sundry how 'we 'ad it 'tuffer' in our time', or looking back through rose-tinted glasses – travelling was more of an adventure in those days. Less knowledge was instantly available for a start, and, without constant connectivity or digitally enabled support, we didn't know as much about the places we were visiting before we went, or even while we were there. We were literally unplugged and 'in the moment' all the time – even more so when cycling slowly through the towns and countryside. Being 'unplugged' is an experience many wealthy tourists now spend an enormous amount of money to achieve, in our 'always on' digital age – we had it for over three months on the Continent and, while at the time it didn't seem unusual, it now ranks as a rare privilege.

Our trip was also important for us personally in many ways, in that it gave us an experience that would stay with us forever. More importantly, it proved to be pivotal in our relationship, and culminated two years later, on the tenth of May, in a church in Harrow, when Jenny and I made the ultimate commitment to one another. Reflecting from nearly forty years on, with two adventurous and grown-up children of our own, and a very happy life in Sydney, we learnt some valuable life lessons – look for the good in people and you will often find it; be positive and open to new ideas and influences; and, seek external input, but follow your own path and trust your instincts. They stood us in good stead on that trip; have been the basis for a wonderful partnership, and a mantra that I have followed during my entire life.

With the benefit of hindsight, I'm also very appreciative of the impact this relatively short trip had on our psyche at the time. It opened our minds to the limitations of viewing everything through the lenses of our homelands, and the possibilities of taking a more global view of the world. It's certainly true that, going into the trip, I was an enthusiastic participant and even propagator of the Englishman's stereotypical European clichés – the French are arrogant, the Italians are flash, the Germans have no sense of humour, the Swiss are boring, and the Dutch are … well, they're the Dutch. It's also true that we did see more than enough instances of behaviour that would support those biases, and that if we had wanted to take a negative view, we could have come away with all those stereotypes reinforced, with multiple examples.

I wasn't above using those classic stereotypes in humour from time to time, in good-natured banter – as indeed the citizens of those countries were of the English in return. Fortunately, Jenny and I were, and are, both positive people. It had been fun to highlight some of the idiosyncrasies we were observing along the way on that trip, but one of the points of the adventure had been to explore different cultures and embrace them for what they were, rather than what they were not. This was never a problem for Jenny with her typical Australian openness. And, for this Englishman, I had decided I would try to be more global in my outlook, and specifically, add a touch of the Italian philosophy, by aspiring to:

'*Mangia bene, ridi spesso, e ama molto*,' – 'Eat well, laugh often, and love much.'